America's Little Black Book

The birth and birthright of America's offspring

*A discourse about the human beings
who were bred in America to be slaves,
our people's abandonment,
our continuing lack of leadership,
and an investigation into
the persistent aftereffects of slavery*

By Norris Shelton

Published by American Slaves, Inc.
Louisville, Kentucky

Web site: www.SlavesUSA.com

ISBN-13: 978-0-976541-70-7 (hc)
ISBN-10: 0-9765417-0-X (hc)

ISBN-13: 978-0-976541-71-4 (pbk)
ISBN-10: 0-9765417-1-8 (pbk)

Library of Congress Control Number: 2005901617

Edited by James E. Reed

Illustrations by Wes Kendall

Book design by Alfred Moreschi

Printed in the U.S.A.

First printing, April 2005
10 9 8 7 6 5 4 3 2 1

9/22/13

America's Little Black Book

To Rosey

From
Morris Shelton,
Your friend

To my mother and father,
Emma and Samuel Shelton

S alt of the earth best describes my parents. My mother was known for her charismatic charm, but she was unyielding when it came to the truth. My father was the wisest, brightest, 'uneducated' person I have ever known.

Together, they made me understand that learning the truth is all the education a decent person needs. They taught me that speaking the truth, in the face of disaster, is all the weapon a God fearing person needs. My parents wielded the truth like a mighty sword.

About the Author and the Book

Norris Shelton is an independent entrepreneur who has long been a member of the Louisville, Kentucky, business community. This book contains what he has learned concerning his racial uniqueness. Mr. Shelton believes that this book could serve as a guide for those who are identified as the leaders of the inner-city people. He further believes that a different look at slavery, through optimistic eyes, would give black inner-city youths a clearer understanding of America and of their immediate surroundings and simultaneously instill an enduring pride in these youngsters.

Mr. Shelton states: "If African American leaders are serious about promoting growth among their people, they need to bond tighter with their people and better understand America. They must become aware of how America operates behind the scenes. To understand what influences the racial growth of some American groups, and the lack of growth of others, these leaders must start at the beginning of the United States of America and compare the descendants of slaves' disregarded history to that of other racial groups that now reside in America, but whose foreparents weren't slaves. They will see right away that it is the 'shared' mentality of an ethnic group that dictates their growth in the human race."

No matter what your race, or what race you think you belong to, it's incumbent upon you to understand Mr. Shelton's argument on the persistent aftereffects of slavery in America, and that you be aware of what lies ahead. His enlightening revelations could be the solution to inner-city problems that our country's leaders have been searching for, but overlooking.

The illustrations and conclusions herein were derived from realistic assessments and sensible, racial parallels — there are no hidden agendas. ❖

Table of Contents

Acknowledgements

Special thanks to James Halvatgis, James Reed and Henry Owens; they challenged, directed and encouraged me in what turned out to be a wonderful, heartfelt undertaking.

Without Jim, Jim and Hank, this book couldn't have been written. When they realized my determination to help my people, they didn't back down from helping me. And, when things got tough and I couldn't see my way, they encouraged me not to back down.

CHAPTER I

The Forgotten People

(The legalities of an 'uncivilized' society)

The supposition that American Slaves were released from slavery, properly, is reminiscent of events when Americans assumed the Korean War was over. As odd as it sounds, in the fall of the year 2000, Secretary of State Madeleine Albright made a visit to the Koreas to start negotiations to *end* the Korean War. Armed combat has been over for decades, but *formally* North Korea and South Korea are still at war. The paperwork that would have brought an end to the war, officially, was never completed and signed. This paperwork would have shown that both North and South Korea had settled upon the conditions spelled out in the agreement.

Leadership incompetence during the Korean War is suggestive of what happened to American Slaves after the Civil War. The slaves were turned loose, but the legal formalities

"History teaches us that our American Civil War was fought to free some 4 million slaves. Yet, they were never formed into a cohesive body; their future was never planned, and their freedom was never documented in the declaration of peace, or the statement of surrender."

that would have protected their freedom and guaranteed a future, peaceful coexistence between the guilty and the innocent, were left flapping in the wind.

History teaches us that our American Civil War was fought to free some 4 million slaves. Yet, they were never formed into a cohesive body. Their future was never planned and their freedom was never documented in the declaration of peace or the statement of surrender. This missing evidence shows that American slaves weren't freed properly.

Legally and ethically, the most detailed records of all, at the conclusion of the war, should have been the documentation that outlined the slaves' freedom — *that's why the Civil War was fought.*

The mental damage that was done to slaves during slavery, and nothing being done about our people's condition since slavery, tells us that the descendants of slaves are not yet mentally or morally free. Descendants of slaves are still relegated to the lower end of the same society that enslaved our ancestors and has always oppressed our people.

Until the American legal system confronts the slavery cover-up, *formally* admits to the wrong of slavery, and then declares all descendants of slaves free, *in writing*, American Slaves will continue to be *legally, mentally, and morally* enslaved. To be truly free, the descendants of slaves must have a written declaration outlining their freedom. This certification must be backed up by an acceptable 'constitutional' program, which will guarantee that freedom. And even this will not completely free the slaves. After these steps are taken, we must systematically address our inherited racial unawareness intelligently.

Deceiving the American slaves into thinking they were free, without devising a plan to assimilate them into mainstream American wasn't emancipation; it was the biggest miscarriage of justice in American history, and now it is being deliberately disregarded.

Parallels and continuations

Slavery is such a broad, yet rarely discussed, subject it's hard to know where to start or what to compare it to, so we may as well go straight to what seems to be on everyone's mind — "reparations for slavery." Throughout the ghetto, there is controversy over our being termed "African Americans" and rumors of a reparations war because of slavery. Slave leaders who caused these rumors could be moving too fast and in the wrong direction.

Because of one-sided assumptions, no one has taken the time to even question whether the American slaves were adequately freed or not — many just assume we were. I can relate to this lackadaisical attitude because, before I was awakened to the overlooked obvious, this was my mindset, too.

The question arises: How do I know my forebears weren't really freed from slavery? Because the Civil War was fought over a hundred years ago, yet present-day descendants of slaves are still being adversely affected by our ancestors' enslavement.

Those who are leading the reparations charge should slow down and take a closer look at slavery; they should think harder about what they are doing and then proceed *cautiously*. Pursuing reparations for slavery, while there is even the slightest possibility that our people are *still enslaved*, is a backward move. A 'negotiated freedom' should come first because that's when the rules outlining our reparations for slavery would be drawn up, clearly explained, and then made public. I wonder, do the attorneys who are intent on winning reparations through the courts realize that, in order to make humans into slaves and then force them to accept slavery, those people must undergo a mental transformation? Have these leaders thought about what this could mean to our people, perpetually?

Our ancestors' mentality was transformed on American soil for the sole purpose of making them slaves. Since I am descended from slaves whose slave mentality was fabricated in America,

I logically conclude that I, too, am an 'American Slave,' but others with the same heritage may not recognize or accept this. Not many descendants of slaves have the presence of mind to take an unbiased look *deep* within their person and ask themselves honestly just who they really are. Well, I did. What I saw confused me at first, then it made me angry. However, after thoughtful deliberation about my 'person,' my confusion was cleared up; my anger subsided, and my life has been changed evermore for the better. It took a while, and I underwent much soul-searching and a period of maturing mentally, but now, I'm proud to be an American Slave.

African American leaders and our country's white leaders have yet to realize who descendants of slaves are. After the many name changes we as a group have had, it would appear at least one of our prestigious colleges that boast creating brilliant minds would have looked into our existence. It seems they would want to know why American Slaves have had several name changes. It's also strange why the American political system hasn't seen fit to question the identity of the offspring of those dark-skinned humans who were enslaved in America — not even when our ethnic name is changed. Personally, I would like see our proper identity *publicly* debated.

Without thinking, most Americans presume that descendants of slaves are "African Americans" because our leaders address each other as such and, now, *so do whites*. The average person doesn't realize this notion was subconsciously embedded in our minds over the years. This false identity helps keep slavery cloaked in obscurity. If ever slavery is completely and successfully covered up, the descendants of slaves can forget about equality, getting justice, obtaining true freedom, or knowing why other American groups treat us as if we are inferior.

To better understand what influences the average white American's manner of free thinking and the descendant of slaves' mentality concerning slavery, it's necessary to look at slavery with an open, untainted mind. This is easier said than done because many slave leaders are closed-minded but won't admit to it. At the same time, white leaders are prejudiced but may not know it. The difficulty of getting at the truth of slavery is that time, shame, and misconception has tainted most Americans' opinions of slavery.

When we look at slavery without our normal prejudices and inherited shame, the truth becomes clear — Slaves and slavery did exist in America and white Americans owned and abused American slaves during slavery. When slaves were turned out into the world they were ignorant, alienated, and destitute and, as of yet, none of these inherited conditions have been adequately addressed or debated. Therefore, it's common sense to conclude they have never been corrected. Still, the average American chooses to believe that the descendants of those abandoned slaves aren't still slaves; that abuse, discrimination and evolution have transformed American slaves into African Americans.

"The vast majority of Americans, white and black, think American slavery is past tense, and that it is "water over the dam," and we should just "move on." I strongly disagree: Slaves are certainly not past tense. We're still right here, right where we have always been — enslaved in America — once visibly, but now, invisibly."

To give slavery the necessary thought it deserves, we must stop assuming and start thinking. Clear thinking will allow us to examine the thick layer of shame that surrounds slavery so we can get at the whole truth. Only then will we be able to see clearly enough to put slavery into perspective.

Most people I talk to view the word "slave," as it relates to the descendants of slaves, as disgraceful. They say 'slave' sounds too terrible to be used in relationship to present day human beings — *especially those of us who are descended from slaves.*

The vast majority of Americans, white and black, think American slavery is past tense; that it is "water over the dam" and we should just "move on." I strongly disagree. Slaves are certainly not past tense. We're still right here, right where we have always been — enslaved in America — once visibly, but now, invisibly. To be precise, the physical side of slavery is a past tense action, and the shameful act that is being covered up or treated as old news, was most certainly, disgraceful — but not the slaves themselves!

Slavery is not over

Understand that the information herein is not written in anger. Neither is this information intended to incite, cause rage, or embarrass the victims of slavery. This book is written with love, both for my people and my country. My intent is to provide a straightforward overview of the progression of American slaves, from slavery up until present. My purpose is to shed some light on gloom and open all Americans' minds to the light of truth. Only then will we understand that the 'darkness of slavery' was the process through which a new nation — the American Slaves nation — was born.

When the heinous act of rape produces a healthy, normal child, that child shouldn't be ashamed of who he or she is — nor should the child be made to carry any shrouded shame derived from the rape. The shame belongs to the perpetrator of the rape.

Once I realized I am an American Slave, a descendant of those who were physically in bondage in America, I asked myself: Why are we, the descendants of slaves, ashamed of who we are? Why are we made to forever pay for our racial population being raped into existence? Why are people like me kept in a suppressed state at all times? Personally, I am not a negative, so why is who I am and what I have become, racially, a negative?

If the slaves of old had been freed from slavery correctly, this book wouldn't matter. But "American Slave" is my essence. Denying my heritage won't finish freeing my people, and it won't make me a better person.

American Slaves' purporting to be African Americans hasn't benefited our masses in the least. It only benefits those of us who have special talents, or those who can be used to make more money for whites without letting on who they really are. Average American Slaves are still not allowed to fully and openly participate in the American mainstream.

In order for all descendants of slaves to participate fully in America, we must first salvage some meaningful benefit from our heritage of slavery. For this to happen, our leaders must rethink American Slaves' position in America. Our sector of the American population must undergo a mental transformation. We must do a complete about-face and get a proper restart. This won't be easy because the first step in our 'turnaround' is to reexamine our identity. We are descendants of American Slaves — not African Americans.

American Slaves achieving a mental makeover will be difficult because of our innate racial unawareness and the divisiveness that we inherited; nonetheless, a restructuring is necessary for our survival. Some African American leaders will say that too much time has passed and too much vital information has been overlooked for descendants of slaves to become a viable, cohesive force of people. Others will say that our racial ignorance has already solidified; that we are just a lost race of dark-skinned people. Well, excuses won't get the job done. No group of people can achieve true freedom until it first stands collectively as a unit.

To better understand the descendants of slaves' quandary, we must understand what causes a slave mentality, and then we must understand how this state of mind works. Consequently, we must start when our people's mentality was formed — during the era of American Slavery. ❖

Chapter 2

Instructions for Slave-makers

(*A most delicate procedure*)

American Slaves were vital to the success of America, but thus far America is, and always has been, callous toward American Slaves.

During slavery, and even until this day, conniving schemers from among our very own people have maneuvered their way into leadership positions. Tragically, too many are allowed to retain their status, even as they repeatedly make unintelligent decisions that cause lamentable blunders. These missteps cause the descendants of slaves to be continually discriminated against or just disregarded altogether.

"Whites arrived at a solution: It is easier to make a single mind accept slavery than an entire, ethnic group of people who are standing together physically and who have a shared, free mentality."

To see the entire picture, we must take an overall look at America from her existence. It is necessary that we understand why the birth of American Slaves was necessary to the building of America. What follows is an interpretation of the other side of our short, almost nonexistent history, by an American Slave who realizes the true nature of his own identity.

The journey begins:

Like any trip, the first step is the hardest. So, open your minds, put your thinking cap on, and try to leave your prejudices behind.

The seeds for the United States of America were planted, so to speak, when whites invaded a new land. This incursion was commercially motivated. The Indians occupying the land, not understanding the finer points of commercial greed, welcomed the whites with open arms. By the time they realized the whites' intentions, it was too late. They found themselves being taken over. Unequipped for advanced warfare, the Native Americans tried to put up a fight, using crude weapons, and even cruder tactics, but they were no match for white technology. The invaders had dynamite, rifles, hand guns, fire-breathing cannons, and assorted other weapons; above all, they knew tried and proven battle tactics.

The Indians had never been around resourceful whites before — they never had a chance.

The creating of a new, servile workforce

After securing the new land, developing it became a labor problem. Because, in order for the American plan to become a successful venture, a strong work force was needed; perhaps slavery was inevitable. The Indians were perfect candidates for subjugation. However, the conquerors found out that, even though dominated, the Indians were bound together as a free-minded people. They were too proud to become slaves for the whites.

The stubborn mindset of the Indians created a major setback, but it also presented a grand business opportunity for scheming whites with creative minds. Whites traveled abroad and captured dark-skinned humans to work, but it was soon discovered that these captives were also too proud to be slaves. They, too, had free mentalities, which meant they, like the Indians, were of no commercial value to whites. This is where brute force, superior weaponry, and white creativity came into play again.

Whites recognized that the Indians were strong, so long as they were together, and they were together because they pos- sessed a joint mentality. The Indians couldn't save their land from falling into the conquerors' hands, but their deep-rooted, strength-in-numbers mindset kept them from "accepting" slavery. The Indian's basic state of mind and tribal pride was properly joined when the various Indian nations were initiated — long before the whites came.

Whites arrived at a solution: It is easier to make a single mind accept slavery than an entire, ethnic group of people who are standing together physically and have a shared, free mentality.

> *"To overcome the free-mentality setback, whites devised a merciless course of action that was driven by greed. They programmed the offspring of their dark-skinned captives' initial mentality for servitude instead of 'free will.'"*

To overcome the free-mentality setback, whites devised a merciless course of action that was driven by greed. They programmed the offspring of their dark-skinned captives' *initial* mentality for servitude instead of 'free will.' This step by step procedure included delivering slaves to induction centers where they were physically separated from each other.

This stopped our foreparents from standing together as an ethnic unit and, at the same time, it split their tribal mentality. Once fully estranged, slaves were publicly traded at slave auction blocks, along with animals, *as if they, themselves, were mere animals.* This closely related, dehumanizing experience with common livestock was done to take away their human pride and forever deprive these unfortunates of their true individuality.

The initial separating of these dark-skinned beings from each other was crucial to the success of slavery. Their physical division resulted in their becoming mentally dissociated, also. This caused individual offspring of the original American Slaves to be born and bred without the normal family ties, or family setting. Young slaves had neither family security nor 'strength in numbers.' All slaves were considered animals and not recognized as a part of any human family. This caused the descendants of slaves to evolve into a divided people whose roots are firmly planted in slavery, *in America.*

If captured slaves were from the same homeland, they were soon separated. Their offspring were born into slavery and disconnected parentally. Here again, they were never told where their people came from. If the older slaves did know where they came from, separation caused the masses of slaves to forget as generations of younger slaves emerged and were further divided, and as older slaves died off. Continued separation eventually caused slaves to no longer comprehend their origin.

From birth, slaves were forced to learn only what was necessary for them to be good slaves. When slaves were sold they were sent to different locations, but they were never told where they were being taken and, geographically, they didn't know where they had been. Slaves weren't allowed to share in the slavery paper trail.

The offspring of slaves had no idea who their foreparents were. Sometimes, they didn't even know who their immediate parents

Instructions for Slave-makers

were; therefore, they couldn't appreciate who their foreparents were as a people. In due course, slaves could no longer tie themselves directly to any roots, except slavery. This tells us two things: The slaves' family succession chain leading up to slavery was callously, but successfully, disconnected, and that the slave mentality was ingrained into our nation at the 'root of our being.'

> *"Young slaves had neither family security nor 'strength in numbers.' Not being a recognized part of any human family caused the descendants of slaves to evolve into a divided people whose roots are firmly planted in slavery, in America."*

Having no details of their actual being and no family sequence to draw from or rely on, newborn, 'dark-skinned-humans' were methodically 'force-fed' information that they were animals. As decades passed, this false data thoroughly confused slaves and reinforced their ignorance. Slave masters freely, and openly, abused their slaves. This was done to intimidate slaves and cultivate an underlying, perpetual fear of all whites in all slaves.

In their daily lives, the totality of the slaves' information intake, concerning their person, was that they were livestock — merely animals. From birth to death, masters treated slaves as domestic property. Receiving no further information over the years to contradict this influx of damaging data, slaves eventually believed they were animals. With the passing of time, whites successfully transformed humans beings into slaves who had no understanding of their own being.

This book is intended to let the descendants of slaves know that, even though slavery was a cruel, illegal act against humanity that was intended to perpetuate itself, to whites this wasn't personal — it was business. At that time, America needed slaves. ❖

13

Chapter 3

Made in America

(The creation of a mindset)

During slavery, slaves were considered plantation livestock and thought of as property, as were domestic animals. From birth, slaves were prepared mentally for a life of physical servitude, bred for endurance, and mentally trained to do tasks according to the slave owner's profitability expectations.

Top of the line, physically-fit slaves who were skilled at doing specific tasks could be sold for higher prices. Therefore, the slave master controlled his slaves' reproduction. Inherent aggression and hostile behavior patterns were altered in all slaves. From birth, slaves were trained to be obedient, deferential and subservient. This created in them the slave mentality necessary for a life of servitude.

The docile persona of slaves and the slaves' fear of the mas-

"Each slave, no matter his bloodline — even slaves that were fathered by the master — was trained to fear, respect, and trust all whites, but to disrespect and connive against each other. This indoctrination of fear and malicious confusion created in slaves a new mindset, causing them to have a subservient approach to life."

llowed slave masters to freely use sexual intercourse to mix
their blood with their slaves' blood. Some did this simply for personal gratification, and others to increase their herds, but when
the two peoples' blood mixed, it caused the masses of slaves to
have a distinctly different appearance. Adding to the mix, a portion of the very founding fathers of America chose to become
some of the founding fathers of American Slaves.

Maternal Love Void

Infant slaves didn't belong to the natural parents but to the
slave master. Babies were routinely separated from the parent
and soon put under the master's rule. This immediate parental
separation took away the channel that supplies knowledge of self.

Because of the high value of slaves, their owners kept records
of when they were born, purchased, traded, sold, died, or were
slain. All new owners received documented proof of slave owner-
ship. When owners bred their slaves, they kept financial records
of their profit and bloodline records of their chattel; yet, when
slaves were supposedly freed, they didn't receive any documentation of their family trees. This kept them ignorant of who they
were, thereby keeping their racial succession chain disconnected.

Being openly misled from their existence caused the
American Slaves, as a community of people, or as a racial family, to take root in rich American soil. However, because they
were considered animals and made to believe they were not
human, they started evolving uninformed of their true person.
The absence of accurate information, and the ingestion of bogus
data that was planted into slaves then, is causing our sector of
the human race to evolve in ignorance yet today. This ignorance
was not apparent to those slaves who were Uncle Toms then
and, evidently, it is not apparent to our leaders even today.

As a result of the illegal introduction to life in a forcefully
controlled environment, and by never having their racial begin-

ning properly explained to them, the American Slaves' overall mentality evolved slowly and developed at a lesser pace than that of other ethnic groups. To reinforce ignorance in slaves, they could be killed for trying to access even basic information that is vital for normal, mental growth.

The white slavers' business plan was simple — supply much needed slaves to America and, in so doing, make a handsome profit. The overall strategy was much more complicated and a lot harder to achieve because of the amount of time involved in mind manipulation. The slave master's ultimate goal was to make humans less human by creating a slave mentality in dark-skinned humans that whites could control. To accomplish this, when slaves were captured they were chained and brutalized until they were 'broken.' When offspring were born they were raised in a dehumanizing, slave environment; slavery was all they ever knew. It was their 'being' and their sole purpose "for being" on earth.

The breeding ground of slavery was not only perverse and immoral, it was outright evil. It involved influencing the innocent minds of dark-skinned humans by wicked, white humans with crass commercial intention.

The slave master continually severed his newborn chattels' parental connection, eventually eliminating any underlying last gasp of racial pride and communal love, and destroying any hope for the future. Inherently drained of hope, void of ethnic love, and disconnected parentally, infant slaves were introduced by their master to their first look at life, their first remembered experience of fear and violence, a different appearance, and an entirely different language. Slave masters knew these ingredients would dictate slaves' behavior and future way of life.

Each slave, no matter his bloodline (even if fathered by the master) was trained to fear, respect, and trust all whites but to disrespect and connive against each other. This indoctrination of fear and malicious confusion created in slaves a new mindset, causing them to have a subservient approach to life. Once properly trained to be subservient and meek, these humans were introduced to the world as slaves. They were marketed in the commercial arena as 'animals' that were bred for strength and endurance, and trained to serve white masters.

Food for thought

The Civil War was fought to end slavery in America and, in one sense, it did. Slave masters was forced to turn their slaves loose. Therefore, when the War ended, unaware Americans *presumed* "slavery" ended, but let us take a closer look, so we can draw a commonsense conclusion: The war ended, but slaves didn't evaporate — they kept right on living, multiplying, *and* being mistreated. Keep in mind, there is more than one way to 'enslave.' Our foreparents were enslaved physically and mentally. Only the physical chains were removed from the slaves. The virtual chains that held American Slaves mentally bound were never removed — *not even mentioned*. So who were these abandoned people now that the Civil War had been fought in their honor to free them?

> *"Understand: The slave populace was not bred naturally or honorably; our slave nation was raped into existence."*

We must be absolutely clear on this: The war only stopped *individual* slaves from being *physically enslaved* and being *legally* called slaves. It didn't stop and it didn't change the slave mentality forced upon our community of people. Understand, the slave populace was not bred naturally *or* honorably; our slave nation was raped into existence.

History reveals that humans were purchased, captured, or even stolen from their original captors and brought to America. Here they were forced to breed, physically. This we have always taken for granted. What we have been overlooking is that the offspring of these humans were disconnected parentally and indoctrinated into a subservient state of mind that was designed by the slave master. This tells us that slaves were also 'mentally-bred' — that is, indoctrinated with a slave mindset. With the passing of time, they became a new breed of people *mentally*. They became slaves, bred without honor, through habituation, using intense mental training and forced psychological exercises. The Civil War caused the physical chains to be removed from the slaves; however, it didn't undo the slave mentality. So, who were these people?

A new race is born

If we open our minds and look at the overall picture, objectively, we will begin to understand basic, human evolution. When we add purpose, and then consider the passing of time, we will understand that these dark-skinned humans were intentionally given a newly designed mindset. Armed with this latest information, we must also conclude that American Slaves were made into a new breed of people — born out of slavery. If we take into account the method in which this new state of mind was installed racially, we must also conclude that American Slaves' mental condition and racial position in America was *intended to be permanent*. However, it doesn't have to be. Now that we are beginning to understand what is hampering our cultural advancement, we can put forth the necessary effort to move our group forward.

The destruction of the slavery paper trail, whether deliberate or simply by neglect, made it impossible to convict those responsible for slavery. However, white Americans *control America*. Whites raped our group into existence and then intentionally instilled ignorance into our being. Once satisfied with their product they sold us in the marketplace as animals. America is completely responsible for our very creation and our plight. America owes 'American Slaves.'

The aftereffect

The process of "mentally breeding" human beings at the same time they were being physically bred, was applied to slaves across the board according to the masters' whims. Selective physical breeding caused most slaves to be stronger, swifter, and more agile. However, the slaves' preplanned 'status' that was planted into slaves during their 'mental breeding' caused the bulk of slaves to have lower aptitudes in certain areas and different interests in others. This adverse way of thinking still affects the descendants of slaves today. During slavery, it allowed the master to own slaves' physical bodies, manipulate their minds, work them as if they were animals, and sell them as livestock.

Today, this inherited mentality has handicapped our leaders; they aren't able to recognize our racial deficiency. The trickle-down from weak, unaware leadership has allowed low esteem to be bred into our people. Low esteem is the parent of a welfare mentality.

Supply, demand and remand

The reason slavery wasn't personal but business is because, in the world of commerce, if some*thing* is needed or wanted, it is purchased or manufactured. When someone is needed, he or she is hired. In the same vein, when something or someone loses its value and because it is not good business practice in the business arena to possess items that have no value, it is usually sold, fired, or thrown away. Slaves couldn't be fired. They weren't employees; they were 'commercialized' possessions. Slaves, like other material possessions were 'manufactured' or either bought and sold, never hired and fired.

When the War Between the States ended, slaves lost their commercial value. Now they couldn't be bought and sold anymore. Having no marketable worth in a commercially driven arena, and because there was no personal sentiment on the part of the slave masters, slaves were simply discarded. No justice was dispensed for the crime of slavery. No plans were drawn up for these abandoned slaves' future, even though they were the only victims of a manmade, living hell. They were just tossed out on their own into a commercial world that thought of them as inferior. They were now on their own, responsible for their own well-being, yet largely ignorant of the world around them. After a lifetime of turmoil and abuse, our foreparents were just pushed out onto the side of the road. This was their American freedom.

To all but the most callous, our beginning seems horrible (and it was) but nonetheless, it did happen. America became a successful venture, so slavery did serve its purpose. We did survive, and now it is time to move on, but we *must* move in the right direction.

I don't believe it's too late for American Slaves to become a better, successful people. To excel, we must use to our advantage this new understanding of who we are.

Compared to other ethnic groups, American Slaves are a young, new people. Our people's racial mentality is just starting to be shaped. We are at the proper age to start budding. It is not only up to American Slaves to get off to a good start on their journey to freedom, it is the duty of America, our mother country, to help us as we learn to crawl. Effort by all will ensure the descendants of slaves growing up and maturing naturally.

I deeply believe if descendants of slaves are made aware of our true being, and if our innate slave mentality is addressed properly, our outlook will reform and our development will begin in earnest.

The question arises: Why do I think our racial ignorance can be cured after all of this time? Just because no one has tried to help American Slaves doesn't mean we are beyond help. Keep in mind the only time our racial mentality was ever addressed was during slavery when whites forced us into our passive mindset, and at the present time when we must straighten it out. ❖

CHAPTER 4

Destroying the Paper Trail

(It doesn't always destroy the evidence!)

The destruction of the slavery paper trail, combined with the slaves' separation, and laws banning them from knowing how to read and write, resulted in the American Slaves having no documented family tree and no recorded or accurate record of their history.

It's doubtful that more than a handful of descendants of slaves could come up with documentation proving their heritage because there is very little meaningful documentation of slavery. In a commercial society, proper documentation is essential, that's how the American system works and why, legally, 'slaves' don't exist! However, all is not lost. American Slaves shouldn't despair, because ignorance and greed caused the paper trail destroyers to overlook the most incriminating evidence of all — we, the descendants of slaves, ourselves.

Well-read unawareness

After slavery was over, slaves were allowed to learn in school. Some of us have even graduated from college. The problem here is — educated slaves are not taught to think about their true history.

Slaves have always learned 'white things.' Schools sprinkle in a little slavery here and there, but they have never taught the descendants of slaves who they really are. This tells me that basic intelligence is still omitted from both our family and formal education. The worst of this blatant omission is the perpetuation of ignorance. Descendants of slaves are allowed to become leaders of their people while they are *ignorant of their own person*. Leaders, both white and black, are standing idly by letting this ignorance be passed on to future generations of slaves, some of whom also will become leaders.

It is because our true history is not taught in schools that younger descendants of slaves don't know how important they are to America. This lack of knowledge takes away from their self-esteem, affecting both black and white children. Neither is taught to understand, or appreciate, the importance of slavery during the formulation of America. Downplaying American Slave 'value' is a major component that keeps the cover-up of American slavery ongoing.

If a full and accurate account of American Slave history had been taught in school slaves, who are attorneys, would have learned long ago that, because slavery was illegal then, *it is still* a legal matter. American Slaves have a birthright and a claim to everything that is America's holdings — *precisely because we are descendants of American Slaves.*

Reparations or complications?

When viewed with an open mind should reparations for slavery come down to a court battle, African American attorneys, who are filing, might not be properly prepared to argue the American Slaves' case. African American attorneys are taught 'law,' but from their dialogue it's obvious they don't understand 'ethnicity.'

If African American, or even white, attorneys desire to *properly* represent us, they must learn every aspect of slaves, slavery, and our racial group being born to America. If any attorney, no

"Slaves have always learned 'white things.' Schools sprinkle in a little slavery here and there, but they have never taught the descendants of slaves who we really are."

matter the nationality, were to step into a courtroom to represent us and not know all about what went into the making of slavery and us being slaves, they could be walking into a well-baited trap. Lawyers for reparations are going to have to present their case to the most brilliant, white minds in America, including some of our brightest Uncle Toms — *because that's who they'll be up against.*

Most African American lawyers presume they are thinking and talking ethnically when they plea for African Americans, or come to the aid of a black person who has been abused by whites. If they studied themselves, they would realize they are simply parroting what someone else said, saw, thought, or wrote, or what they read in a law book that is similar to the situation they are involved in. That's not ethnic thinking. In the case of American Slaves, that's blatant failure to acknowledge racially-related facts. If they studied most of their 'racial' cases, they would realize they are arguing for individual slaves who think they are African Americans — not the American Slave nation.

If African American attorneys wish to help the descendants of slaves, they must learn to have fresh, new thoughts of their own concerning slavery, because American Slaves are a new nation. They must rely on realizing their true being and connecting with our foreparents, mentally, and then indulging in healthy, open debate in regard to our true identity. Once dialogue is started, it shouldn't be too difficult to deduct who we are because, when you think about it, we descendants of slaves are everywhere and easily recognizable.

Scholarly slaves have always been involved with American history, but they are denied access to proper information concerning American Slave history. One sided history is encouraged and also taught in our schools from the lowest level to the highest. This omitted, important information has caused the average descendants of slaves to be indifferent about their person.

Emerging slaves, not being taught our history, and older slaves, having all but forgotten about our race's past, could wind up being costly because *our people are not yet legally free.*

It's necessary to understand America in her 'commercial infancy' to appreciate American slaves' significance to the American economy during slavery. Therefore, we must journey back into time because when a 'real slave' looks at slavery from a legal point of view and uses moral judgment, concealed facts that African American lawyers haven't even considered become surprisingly visible.

Civil War?

The North and South were involved in fierce economic competition that would shape America for the future. To gain an advantage, the South started mass breeding slaves openly. Profits from slavery allowed the South to rise in prominence. However, the illegal act of slavery prompted the North to fight the South until they unchained their slaves. Free at last, the slaves scat-

"It's doubtful that more than a handful of descendants of slaves could come up with documentation proving their heritage, because there is very little meaningful documentation of slavery."

tered like barnyard animals left unattended and unfettered.

The Civil War brought an end to the physical side of slavery, but the slaves were never truly freed. They were kicked out of slavery into a world that thought of them as inferior. They were ignorant of their surroundings, destitute, and their mentality, which made them slaves, was never adjusted.

The Union Army's mission didn't include adjusting mentalities, educating slaves, or relocating them. When we look closely at the Civil War with an open mind, we see that, in truth, neither side was in the war to help slaves. We realize it was never intended for slaves, or their descendants, to be a part of America or have a worthwhile interest in America. The South was fighting so they could keep slaves enslaved, and the North was fighting to level the economic playing field because the South had slaves, giving the South an unfair, commercial advantage. ❖

CHAPTER 5

What's My Name?

(The origination of slaves' surnames)

In captivity, slaves were usually called by a first name; this was all they had. Our forebears didn't have last names as we now have. For instance, let's say a slave belonged to Mr. Charles Shelton, owner of the Shelton Plantation, and the slave's name was Sam. When the slave was asked to identify himself, it made little difference that he completely belonged to "Mr. Charlie," or even if he was naturally fathered by Master Shelton, he knew to answer, "I's Big Sam, Massa Charlie's slave, over at the Shelton Plantation." The slave replying, "My name is Sam Shelton, from the Shelton Plantation," was out of the question. If he were to tell the truth, he would say, "I am Sam Shelton, Master Shelton's son, but to the world, even though he sired me, I'm his slave. If there were justice in America for slaves, I would be

> "Descendants of slaves don't know who we are because no one has told us from whence we, as a group, really came nor how we as a people came about. Having so many name changes would indicate that, even though bewildered and disoriented, we are still seeking our true identity."

heir to the Shelton Plantation." Such a brashly stated, simple truth could bring about his death — possibly by his own father's hand.

During slavery, individual slaves were forced into being ignorant of who they were in comparison to other human beings. The trickle-down from this lack of knowledge is causing American Slaves to grow up in ignorance of our identity in comparison to other peer groups, including our white kinfolk.

In America, it's customary to have a surname; therefore, when the Civil War was over many slaves rightfully assumed their white masters' names, *and that's not all bad*. In fact, this was an opportune occurrence. Being a businessman, I look at slavery from a business point of view. It will be a lot easier to claim our slavery inheritance if we have the same names as the ones who enslaved us. Slavery surnames tell a true, compelling story. It connects us to our true roots — America.

The Importance of a Name

*T*here are documented cases of individuals having their names changed, but it is out of the ordinary for an entire racial group of people to have a name change ever so often. In American Slaves' short history, we have had several.

When slavery was flourishing, *nigger* and *black* were two of many disparagements for slaves. When I was a youngster, slaves were called *colored*. When Dr. Martin Luther King Jr. was leading the descendants of slaves, we were called *Negroes*. *Black* succeeded *Negro* as the major term of self-definition during the Black Power years. In the late 1980s, in the aftermath of a smaller cultural, nationalist movement, African American superseded *black* as a preferred term of self-reference. However, if we start at our beginning back during slavery, our racial name was *slave*.

"It's clear to see that the leadership of American Slaves is confused about where their people's roots are planted."

It's clear to see that the leadership of American Slaves is confused about where their people's roots are planted. To put it bluntly, descendants of slaves don't know who we are because no one has told us from whence we, as a group, really came, or how we as a people came about. Having so many name changes would indicate that, even though bewildered and disoriented, we are still seeking our true identity.

Immediately after the descendants of slaves, or Negroes as we were known in those days, got the right to vote, it seems judicious politicians would have wanted to know every detail of something as important as changing the name of a group of people who were once enslaved in America but are now an integral part of the American infrastructure. If we look at slavery from a lawful point of view, it should have taken an act of Congress, or some other arm of the government, to change the descendants of slaves' names. We are a permanent part of

America and should be represented in our society legally and politically.

If slaves had been properly freed from slavery and then properly reformed as freed slaves, *legally and formally*, our name wouldn't have been changed, unless it was changed lawfully. There would be documentation showing the legal name change, why it was changed, who recommended the change, and who voted in favor of or against the change.

If America were an honorable country and believed in fair play, the descendants of slaves would be recognized as America's only offspring and allowed our proper status. Dumping the American Slaves in their hour of greatest need was a dishonorable act.

Legally, American Slaves' true history and all of our ethnic group name changes, and the reasons for the changes, should be recorded and kept adjacent to the United States Constitution. From a *moral* point of view, slaves should be declared America's first born *in* the Constitution. This didn't happen because, as a rule, criminals don't keep records of their crimes. The U.S. Constitution is our country's record. We don't want to put in writing, in our Constitution, that our country is guilty of heaping injustice upon the innocent. America is just as guilty as any criminals who kidnap, maim, rape, and murder. Slaves were kidnapped and brought to America where they were bred to be ignorant and were subjugated, tortured, maimed, even murdered. These crimes were illegal then, and they still are.

To make my argument that descendants of slaves are still slaves and not Africans, nor African Americans, let us deal with the crime of kidnapping in a broader sense. Usually when people are abducted and then later released they are, in most cases, returned to their loved ones, or they go back to being who they were before they were captured. This tells us that if the progeny of those slaves who were captured in Africa, and then enslaved in America, had still been Africans at the close of the Civil War, they would have gone back to their respected African tribes legally and with full honor. Our predecessors were no longer 'Africans.' They were now a mixture of nationalities. Through selective breeding and mind manipulation, they were transformed into slaves. They were a brand new people because they had been given a complete mental, physical, and emotional makeover.

After the Civil War, whites told slaves they were a newly freed people, so that's what they believed. In reality, they were naive, abandoned slaves. Being sorely uninformed, whites tricked slaves into thinking they were 'free Negroes.' This is when the American Slavery cover-up was started. Whites couldn't legally call slaves "slaves" anymore. It would not only describe the crime, it would point out the evidence; consequently, they started calling us Negro. In several languages — Latin, Spanish and Portuguese, among others — Negro means *black*.

"If America were an honorable country, and believed in fair play, the descendants of slaves would be recognized as America's only offspring and allowed our proper status. Dumping the American Slaves in their hour of greatest need was a dishonorable act."

American Slaves is a newborn nation that was bred by white Americans. America is our parent country and our motherland. By law, it was, and still is, America's duty to *officially* name us. That's the first thing a parent does to her newborn when they enter this world. The same should also apply on a larger scale to a newborn *ethnic* group.

However, to put our identity into 'proper' perspective, America did name us. Our 'mother country' named us slaves! Like it or not, that's our "birth name."

American Slaves are a case study of how a brand new, different nation was created. The world is just now becoming conscious of it. The descendants of slaves must also be made aware that the slave mentality, which controls our racial destiny, was altered intentionally because, at that time, America didn't need African Americans or any other 'free' Americans — America needed slaves. The Indians wouldn't cooperate, so here we are.

We have now evolved into an easily recognizable group of American people. If freedom is ever to be obtainable for all descendants of slaves, we must know and accept the truth of who we are. True, there are some African Americans in America; they are legally attached to Africa. Descendants of American Slaves have no attachment to Africa. All of our ties are to America, our mother country. Fooling our people into thinking they are Africans, and inducing them to change their names to sound African, is nothing more than another attempt at covering up the crime of slavery.

What's the point?

*A*t this juncture, I would like to make my position clear: Since America has been in existence, there has been only one ethnic group of people created, born, and brought into their mental and racial existence on her soil and under her holdings — the American Slaves. The point is we are America's only child — *but we don't know it!*

To prove my point, let me share with you our *proper* identity and how all of these epithets came about: Our foreparents were bred to be slaves, so that's what they were named and what they were called. Before the Civil War, and during the war, they were still called slaves because that's what they were.

When the war was over they were released into degradation, still without honor. They were now *abandoned* slaves because that was their true condition. At that time, whites told us we were Negroes and we accepted that 'handle' because we didn't know any better.

When Dr. King was leading us we still thought we were Negroes, but we were gaining wisdom, because we now had a leader who was not afraid to seek the truth and try to find justice for all *of his people*. Being a moral person, he couldn't be bought off. Seeking "justice for all" cost him his life.

> *"America's only offspring wound up without proper identity, without a leader, and no cultural direction. Drifting aimlessly, we have evolved into confused slaves because we think we are African Americans!"*

America's only offspring wound up without proper identity, without a leader, and no cultural direction. Drifting aimlessly, we have evolved into confused slaves *because we think we are African Americans!*

Whites still call us niggers and blacks — the first verbal slanders they used to remind us we were slaves.

It's thought-provoking, but most descendants of slaves in our inner cities casually call each other *nigger*; yet, the average slave will not allow a white person to call him a nigger. To attest to our racial forgetfulness, slaves don't connect this relaxed name-calling among themselves, and our refusing to let a white person call us niggers as information related to slavery. The average descendants of slaves have no idea why it upsets them so much when a white person calls them a nigger.

Slaves have had many names that are slanderous, but our next *popular* name was "colored" (this was more tolerable, and seemed appropriate because of the "color-variations" in our complexions). But a long while later during one of our movements, someone figured if Caucasians with their own wide variety of lighter skin tints were white, then slaves with their own wide variety of darker skin tints, must be black — and the name quickly caught on. Our leaders disregarded the fact that, at one time, *black* was considered more of a slur name than was *nigger*. Our people accepting black as our racial name now, knowing how much we hated being called *black* then, tells me that once we know the truth of who we are, we will again accept our rightful name. Not only did the word black cease being a racist term, black became our source of enlightenment and ethnic pride because it proudly, but not always accurately, distinguished us from other ethnic groups.

Most modern day slaves had barely gotten used to saying the word black out loud, except when slandering each other, when we underwent something of a silent movement and we were slickly renamed African American.

This time, it appears our racial name was changed with this rationale — if there are French Americans and German Americans (and the list continues), then we must be African Americans. Most descendants of American Slaves have dark skin and tight, curly hair that is similar to dark-skinned Africans, and the majority of us are convinced that the humans who started our slave nation came from Africa. However, with the exception of a few individual slaves who *claim* they can trace their lineage back to Africa, the bulk of the descendants of slaves don't have a known, proven, legal lineage predating slavery, and no documented connection to Africa, whatsoever!

Being called slur names, and having derisive nicknames is as American as apple pie. Consequently, when the descendants of slaves were fallaciously named African Americans, the name stuck, and somehow persists.

"Our seeds were sown on American soil. Any ties we had to Africa, before our ancestors' abduction, were clipped, or cut off at the 'root' during their capture."

I hadn't been in business very long before the advent of the African American designation, and I still didn't know too much about the underlying functioning of America, but one thing I did know, being called an African American wasn't a step up in life for me. I wasn't then, and I have never been, treated like German Americans, Russian, or Italian Americans, not even when I was in the limelight of my business career. I always have been, and still am, treated like I am descended from slaves.

It's clear to me that our leaders are confused. They have, to some extent, forgotten about slavery and who slaves are, and the premeditated hell our ancestors went through, because they have lost sight of who they themselves are. They are passing their forgetfulness, *or ignorance,* on to our descendants, ensuring that our people remain in a disturbed mental state indefinitely if someone doesn't step forward and enlighten all of us to the obvious.

American Slaves can pretend they are African Americans, but we can't "go back to Africa." While the warm bodies that were captured and forced to carry the seeds that gave us our start in the human race, *may well have come from Africa*, we must keep in mind that our African, ancestral, umbilical cord was severed when our progenitors were captured. Any ties we had to Africa, before our ancestors' abduction, were clipped or cut off at the 'root' during their capture. *Our seeds were sown on American soil* — the harvest was slaves! Our ethnic group took *root* on American soil, and was born and bred here in the U.S.A. — not in Africa!

If our leaders would open their eyes, they couldn't help but see that we are the 'yield' of those captured seeds; we are the descendants of those abandoned slaves. If they would open their minds they would understand — we rightfully belong to America. We are American-made!

If doubters should desire to challenge these facts and insist the descendants of American Slaves are still African American, there should be a definite, clear-cut distinction made between the Africans who came to our country seeking their fortunes and being granted a United States visa, or awarded American citizenship, in contrast to those human

> *"At first glance, it appears that the cover-up of slavery is working because, since slavery, little has been, or is being, documented about our progress as a group of people. But, when we go behind the scenes, in the depth of the 'hood, we realize, slavery is not over — at most, it's only "on hold."*

beings whose mentality was bred on *American soil* for the sole purpose of producing warm bodies to become servants or slaves for white Americans.

American history is being written every day, and comprehensive records are being kept concerning the past, but these records are neither detailed nor accurate. They are one-sided because American Slaves are still being left out. It's as if we don't exist. Nothing binding was documented about our origin because our creation, through slavery, was considered disgraceful. Now that I have been racially awakened, I understand why slavery is being covered up. Slavery was, and still is, illegal, and we are not legally free.

At first glance, it appears that the cover-up of slavery is working because, since slavery, little has been or is being documented about our progress as a group of people. However, when we go behind the scenes in the depth of the 'hood, we realize, slavery is not over — at most, it's only "on hold."

American leaders, black and white, are standing by letting the injustice of slavery go unpunished. This makes them responsible for the pressure that builds up in our inner-cities, resulting in racial unrest. They should realize, being coldhearted toward so severe a crime doesn't exonerate our homeland; it only makes knowledgeable slaves think America is a 'lowdown' country.

Maybe those who control America think America has come too far, or that the problem of slavery is too large to solve. I strongly disagree — all is not lost. Slavery is not that far in the past. How could America, the most powerful country in the world, say helping those that she has used, abused, and then abandoned is too big of a problem to solve? It is never too late to do the right thing. If our country's leaders were to deal with these truths honorably and in a timely fashion, they could set the record straight; they could erase the disgrace of slavery. ❖

CHAPTER 6

Captivity and Confinement by Design

(Handed down habit)

To further my argument that slaves were captured and then intentionally bred ignorant, and that the 'slave mentality' that was bred into our forebears still controls the descendants of slaves today, let us look at slavery in conjunction with human incarnation in general. A living organism that is born and lives in its natural, free habitat will not have the same habits or outlook as a being that was born out of rape and then cast directly into captivity.

People who have been caged and enslaved illegally need to understand their unauthorized captivity and illegal detention. It's true that the unfettered and the captive will have some of the same characteristics. Even if they live together until they learn they are poles apart, and why, and then learn how to bridge the distance, they will contin-

"American Slaves' mentality is manmade, not a divine intervention; therefore, the slave state of mind that whites bred into our ancestors to remove their God-given, free way of thinking can be corrected if dealt with properly."

ue to have a dissimilar mentality. They and their offspring will have a different outlook because their group, overall, is treated differently. Since they are viewed differently, they *subconsciously* are put into a different category.

The same goes for humans who have been fashioned into slaves or were born in captivity and destined to be slaves. Their group will not have the same overall mentality as a group of humans who were born free and whose ancestors were free, not until the leadership of the group understands who their group is in comparison to the group who hold the reins of freedom. It is necessary that our leaders understand how the power of freedom is transferred and controlled. Only then will they understand that it is the *combined mentality of our people* that can make freedom work for our culture.

Politicians illustrate they understand what captivity and confinement can do to humans; this is why there are halfway houses for ex-cons and parole officers who supervise them. Human beings who have been captured and made into prisoners need time to deal openly with having been incarcerated. To see the picture more clearly, compare an individual's capture and confinement to that of a community of people being pent-up and, through intense habituation, made to believe they are beasts. Slaves were thought of as beasts, treated as if they were animals, made to believe they were less than human, and then improperly released into a society that hated them. They were then expected to compete for their own survival without any guidance *whatsoever*. The picture clearly shows that American Slaves were captured, confined, misled, kept uninformed, abused, and then abandoned!

I was watching the Oprah Winfrey show during the latter part of the year 2003. She stated that if you throw people away, and keep throwing them away, they will eventually act like people who have been *thrown away*. Ms. Winfrey used the word 'people,' but while I believe she was talking on the individual level, the same logic applies collectively.

Let us compare a thrown away 'person' to American Slaves' entire existence. When slavery was over, slaves lost their commercial value, so they were thrown away. Today's descendants of slaves are nothing more than an extension of our ancestors' ignorance, their enslavement, and also of their abandonment. Thrown away slaves, who are still mentally enslaved, can never be spiritually free until they understand who they are. It is only right that our people should know why and how our division of the human race came about. Withholding our proper identity is a chain that holds us mentally captive today.

Slaves must be taught to appreciate our real value. For this to happen we must be taught the truth, and then we must be strong enough to accept the truth. The truth is *our ancestors were bred to be slaves for white Americans*. I don't know of another way this truth could be told and be factual. To be truly free, we must know why we, the descendants of those same slaves, are still being abused by our 'white controlled establishment' today, instead of being compensated for our foreparents having been abused by this same white controlled system during slavery.

Slavery is an emotional issue; however, I don't have the luxury, or the time to be emotional or angry and I am certainly not going to run from my inherited obligation by claiming that I'm an African American. I am a businessman and an elder of my people; it is my duty to look out for them. I want to ascertain what benefits can be derived from our ancestors being enslaved and then thrown away. Please don't get the wrong impression. I am opposed to human enslavement, period, but I have no other choice but to play the only hand that I was dealt the best that I can. It's my inherited duty as a slave businessperson to discover if slavery might be beneficial to descendants of American Slaves because our ancestors were forced to invest their very lives in it.

There are many questions concerning our identity that need

to be answered. Issues surrounding slavery need to be dealt with to our people's satisfaction. If American leaders have any backbone at all, they will not allow shame, ignorance, and fear to continue destroying the slave nation.

American Slaves' mentality is manmade, not a divine intervention. Therefore, the slave state of mind that whites bred into our ancestors, to remove their God-given, free way of thinking, can be corrected if dealt with properly. It will take time, but it can be done. The first step we must take in order to improve our people's inherited mentality is to recognize the intellectual deficiency among our leaders. To advance our people into the American socioeconomic mainstream, we must gain enough racial intelligence to elect a knowledgeable descendant of American Slaves, *who knows who he or she is*, to lead our people.

Fear may cause some slaves, who are otherwise qualified to lead our people, to balk at leading us. They might think they could be a lamb that is to be sacrificed. However, being the 'sacrificial lamb' will not be the only stumbling block in the pathway to finding a real leader; ingrained ignorance will be the largest one. Whoever leads us must understand how freedom works and what being a legitimate people entails.

In my search for leadership, I interviewed an 'African American' who calls himself a leader. After listening to his argument, I concluded that he wasn't a leader at all but instead an 'Uncle Tom.' His argument was: "All Americans are individuals — we're all Americans now! So what's the big deal, Brother?"

The big deal and the problem with that position is things will continue as they are. Uncle Toms will remain 'house niggers' and keep on selling their people out. Ordinary slaves will keep on getting mixed in at the bottom of all other racial groups, and this includes newly arriving immigrants. We must keep in mind — all it takes to be an *American* is to be born *in* America, or be

"Slave leaders don't want to work together because they cannot envision the possibilities in working together. ... In reality, there has never been a system through which our leaders could work together."

immigrated to America. American Slaves are special, and we must make the most of who we are. We are the only group of people in this world who have the stately distinction of being born in, and to, America. We are descended from those who helped build America from her commencement. *American Slaves are pure American* because no other country but America has ever influenced our racial makeup. This overlooked information is vitally important to our people receiving 'proper' restitution for slavery.

Some might remind us that the Indians were in America first, or that America shaped their racial mentality. This is not so — the Indians were already on the land when the United States of America was started. They were already a formed group and an established population. Whites didn't breed the Indian nation into existence. Their mentality was ingrained long before whites conquered them; that's why whites couldn't make them into slaves. The Indians were conquered by whites, not *bred* by whites.

The United States had no influence on the American Indian's entry into the human race, which is when their people's mentality was formed. On the other hand, America has always *totally* influenced the American Slaves' racial mentality because America didn't defeat the African nation and turn them into slaves, either. America captured individuals, *who most probably were Africans*, and bred their *offspring* into a nation of American Slaves. Our distinct population group didn't even start until America captured human beings on another continent, brought them to America, and then bred their offspring.

Our ancestors were instrumental in formulating the greatest country in the world — America — and our racial group has never been remunerated for our ancestors' forced participation in the lucrative business venture called slavery, nor have we been compensated, or even recognized, for our efforts in the building of America. American Slaves have never been dealt justice nor have we ever been treated fairly by the very *country that we helped build!*

Suppose we keep misleading our young into believing they are African American, instead of American Slaves, for another hundred years. Our slave nation would never get justice. This miscarriage of justice would be on the shoulders of our present day leaders, black and white, for not learning how to reason properly, or think rationally, concerning the many different racial groups now residing in America and, therefore, unknowingly misleading America's only offspring, the descendants of American Slaves.

It is only right that slaves be able to cash in on the fruits of slavery, as did the slave masters. Justice can only be served by slavery paying off for all descendants of slaves, as it paid off for the masters. That will be proper reparations.

Our leaders apparently must not recognize that being slaves is the only card the descendants of slaves have to play. If they understood basic American business at all, they would realize it's our 'ace in the hole!'

Unfortunately, African American leaders aren't yet able to think at this level; presently, they might not understand the message. They, themselves, could become the stumbling block that stands in the way of slave descendants and whites coming together in diplomatic unity. Typically, these leaders are living in luxury, and perhaps comfort has made them weak. They might not be strong enough to admit they are slaves. It's almost certain that, because of their academic pedigrees, they won't admit to being ignorant slaves. If these weak, insecure leaders are allowed to remain in leadership positions and never gain enough commonsense intelligence to realize who they are, they won't seek out their true birthright. Their racial ignorance could lead all slaves to forfeit our American Slaves' heritage.

"It is only right that slaves be able to cash in on the fruits of slavery, as did the slave masters. Justice can only be served by slavery paying off for all descendants of slaves, as it paid off for the masters. That will be proper reparations."

African American leadership is the pits. When Dr. King was assassinated, the remaining leaders got scared. They didn't know which Negro leader was next in line to be murdered. To be on the safe side, they disassociated themselves from 'the struggle' and from being Negroes, and started claiming they were African Americans. Someone must stop them from leading us away from our true identity; not realizing who we are, they're about to give away our heritage. ❖

America's Little Black Book

Chapter 7

Servitude Ingrained

(Hate accumulated)

The longer slaves have been free, the more knowledge we have gained. This accumulated intelligence has given slave descendants an appreciation of how morally in the wrong the original white slave masters were. This realization marks when our deep-seated fear of whites started turning to a slow-burning anger and hate toward them.

Since Dr. King's assassination, American Slaves haven't had leadership with enough nerve or intelligence to figure out what our real grievances are so they can be aired. This hate has been turned inward and allowed to fester. Whites don't realize the slave descendants' dissatisfaction because we have no one to speak up for us. We are a voiceless people, and we are frustrated at not to being able to do anything about the benumbed anger that is building up within our group.

Being frustrated and angry and not knowing why we are inadequately prepared to rise

"Slave leaders don't know how to repair the problem, and peer pressure causes them to be afraid to try any new ideas. They continue using the same old quick fixes that have always failed."

above our present lot in life has caused the majority of our people to be ashamed. We don't recognize that our frustration is a byproduct of this shame because our shame is an intrinsic carryover from slavery. It follows that we are also reflexively ashamed of our foreparents for being slaves.

As of yet, the only release from this pent-up hostility has been in the form of violent, inner-city flare-ups. Slave leaders don't know how to repair the problem, and peer pressure causes them to be afraid to try any new ideas. They continue using the same old quick fixes that have always failed. Being too blind to look for any new solutions, and too closed minded to ask for help, they typically hold futile meetings and shake their fists in the air. Isolated incidents are ordinarily quelled with the usual broken promises.

Homemade lies won't fix the problem. Deception can only pacify the inner-city people's ignorance, temporarily. These short term pacifications cause the real problem — the unconscious shame and hate derived from slavery — to be turned inward to slowly fester until the next flare-up.

Which is stronger, shame, hostility or sound logic?

Right now, I would have to say shame and hostility are winning that contest.

Since the descendants of slaves can't pinpoint each individual white person who is descended from slave masters, we reflexively dislike all whites. That's why hostility sometimes gets out of hand and runs amuck. It was members of the white race who degraded our ancestors and caused our racial shame. This shameful degradation was passed on to us. We see and feel it every day, but because of the systematic way we have been made to forget about our history, we don't fully understand what we are seeing or what we are feeling. Our inherited shame causes us to sense this dreadful feeling came from something we did wrong.

"Color variation is one of the sources of discord that stop the descendants of slaves from standing together as a unit. ... Our complexions vary all the way from whitest white to blackest black, still, we're a distinctively unique group and — with rare exception — easily recognizable."

Slaves have always confused our underlying loathing of whites with our unconscious shame with ourselves. Slaves often let shame overrule racial logic. Some slaves refused to carry on the slave master's name as all offspring are supposed to do. When our people were fallaciously labeled African American, we even learned African names and started naming our offspring names that sounded African. Some slaves even changed their religions — and some cleverly replaced their inherited slave names with an X. This is what Malcolm X, one of our most noted, outspoken leaders did. On many occasions he stated that he was ashamed of the light-skinned complexion he inherited from his white ancestors and of his slave name his black progenitors took on. He couldn't do anything about his complexion, but he swore not to bear his slave name any longer.

Boxer Muhammad Ali had a realization. He changed his slave name and his religion, both at the same time. America doesn't much care for descendants of slaves attempting to control their own destiny. When Ali tried to enlighten other slaves to their shortcomings, it cost him his livelihood. Whites attacked in force, and some of our noted Uncle Toms came out of the woodwork to lend their undying support to whites. Neither Uncle Toms nor whites understand the underlying oppression ordinary slaves feel.

American tradition, ingrained

I am lighter than you — *I'm better than you*. That's the way it has always been in America. Color variation is one of the sources of discord that stop the descendants of slaves from standing together as a unit. The blend of white blood from our white ancestors caused the majority of descendants of slaves to have a lighter skin tone than true Africans. Our complexions vary all the way from whitest white to blackest black. Still we're a distinctively unique group and, with rare exception, easily recognizable. This rich color mixture should bind us together because it tells a convincing story about our past and how our slave nation came about. However, instead of it making us one, it adds to the division among our people. Instead of strengthening, it weakens us. Our leaders don't know how to use the splendor of our being a beautiful, yet multi-hued people, and how our hues came about, to our people's advantage.

How would America look without her beautiful slaves? How would our music sound? What kind of dances would we be doing? What about our different slang language and free-spirited hand shakes? Slaves are the creators of many of America's lifestyles, and we are the most multi-hued flower in the American garden.

During slavery, the lighter skinned slaves, who were descendants of the slave masters, were treated better than the darker skinned field hands. They couldn't be called by the slave master's surname, but they often worked in the master's home and were held in higher regard than the darker of their contemporaries. Until this day, the lighter skinned of us are treated better and afforded more opportunities by other population groups — *and even by our own people!*

Shame has caused slaves to try in every way we can to deny or disconnect ourselves from the darkness of slavery. We have straightened and bleached our hair; we have tried to lighten our skin; we have denied our close kin and some of us even gave up our slave surnames. Now, we are impersonating Africans. Descendants of slaves can never be detached from slavery, from white folk, or from America. And our lesser condition in America will never change as long as our leaders are trying to cover up slavery. Following the path set by our current leaders, we can only grow more ignorant of our history and more alienated from what *should* be rightfully ours. Facts can't be changed by omission, by being overlooked, or because someone calls fact falsehood. Farsighted leaders would not allow the truth of slavery to continue being hushed up, not after they hear the truth and recognize it as such. Leaders who have the capacity to learn from mistakes wouldn't allow this world-known history to continue being omitted from American history.

"The lighter skinned of us are treated better and afforded more opportunities ... even by our own people!"

Individual American Slaves changing their names to sound African won't force our people to automatically become African Americans, and it's not acceptable! It's causing most of our leaders to actually think they *are* Africans, and all of us to forget who we are, comparatively. ❖

CHAPTER 8

African American Historians

(What have they been thinking about?)

S ome descendants of slaves say they are historians. But, in the next breath, they say they are African Americans. Now, how could that be? Technically, the two don't go together. A real historian would know this.

Seems to me our history leaders are unaware of their true identity. This could only mean they are also ignorant of our true history. I can understand a 'white' historian not recording 'slave' history, but this blatant oversight of our 'true being' by slave historians is unacceptable. Think about it: Even though descendants of American Slaves are making their way through history day by day, our history is still inadequately documented — even by those descendants of slaves who call themselves historians. When history is not recorded, it's eventually lost.

> *"Most slaves who claim to be historians derive their information from books that were written by whites — for whites. Our historians are reading and researching what whites have written, but they are not thinking."*

I have talked to descendants of slaves who hold doctorate degrees. Some of these are college professors who profess to be, and truly believe they are, historians. After talking to some of these people and then interviewing some of our high ranking officials, I came to realize the true breadth of slave ignorance. Even our most learned individuals are contributing to keeping all American Slaves ignorant and mentally enslaved.

Slave historians often write misleading books that sell worldwide. In regard to slaves, these books do nothing more than describe blurred events of the past. They never explain who the descendants of slaves are in relationship to other population groups in this world — *and that's what history should be all about!* They don't even tell us who we are in comparison to other groups we reside among in America.

Most slaves who claim to be historians derive their information from books that were written by whites — for whites. Our historians are reading and researching what whites have written, but they are not thinking. They have never thought about what whites have not written, or what hasn't been researched. This is why they have never understood American Slave history because it is purposely not in black and white. Keep in mind, slavery is being covered up; the slavery paper trail was *purposely* destroyed.

Our historians must start actively reconstructing the paper trail that surrounds American Slaves and slavery, so we will have a foundation on which to build. I am not alluding to personal paper trails; many of us have been trying to do that for a long time. I am speaking directly to whatever paper trails we can come up with that describe who we are *as a people* and what happened to us that caused our *group* to evolve in a deficient manner. This shouldn't be too hard to do; it was only a short time ago that our people were discarded from slavery.

In reconstructing the slavery paper trail, our leaders will come to understand our abandonment, continued abuse, and how our people arrived at this juncture. At that time we will begin to understand how to usher in a progressive movement.

Learning made easy

Those who take credit for leading us aren't taking advantage of their professional positions. Most 'African American' ministers, teachers, politicians, and businesspersons are in perfect situations to help our people but, because of their identity crisis, they don't realize this advantage. *They are around white leaders!* Their white counterparts have proven their racial group is among the most powerful, smartest people in the world. Our leaders sit with these same whites every day, all day, at all levels. Nevertheless, they still haven't figured out why and how whites work together for common causes. It's necessary that our leaders learn white tenacity and how to put 'white-resolve' to work cleaning up our inner-cities and developing our people. I am not talking about coming into slave neighborhoods and building more do-it-yourself huts; I am talking about improving our people's position in America.

"Slave historians often write misleading books that sell worldwide. In regard to slaves, these books do nothing more than describe blurred events of the past. They never explain who the descendants of slaves are in relationship to other population groups in this world — and that's what history should be all about!"

To improve our inner cities, we must first elevate the inner-city dweller's mentality. Our leaders must face the fact that the vast majority of the people in our inner cities are descendants of American Slaves. Leaders can't help us until they realize that we are born and bred Americans, not African Americans who by the very definition are immigrants. They must understand our slave nation is a new breed of people *programmed to not work together,* unless a white person is in charge. Ethnic unity is absolutely essential for us to break free.

Working together will allow descendants of slaves to help ourselves and then others in our ethnic group. Our historians, not realizing our peoples' true history, is the reason they cannot explain why our sector of the human race hasn't adequately developed during our short American era. The 'facts' of who we are will allow our politicians to categorize those lingering problems that have always hampered *our* growth.

If our leaders knew the truth, and were to speak it clearly and in *unison,* America would not only hear the cries of our people, white leaders would identify with the message. They then would understand how to truly liberate us without the process destabilizing our country.

I ain't no ignorant slave!

A legitimate leader would know that correcting "weaknesses" among their followers is the first order of business because it would make the overall populace stronger. African American leaders are reluctant to address the most obvious flaw in our group that is keeping descendants of slaves a weak, divided nation — racial ignorance. African American politicians regard this topic to be a "political hot potato."

Most ordinary slaves regard ignorance as a defect in *their* ability to learn, or relate it to *their* being backward or stupid. That

While some might still blurt, "They all look alike to me," the fact is, among ourselves, we appear unable to see what clearly unifies us: our slave heritage.

is not my argument; the ignorance that I am addressing surrounds the American Slaves' nation. Individual slaves can learn, individually. Ours is an ancestral, collective ignorance, an abusive, intellectual deprivation that was ingrained at the *origin* of our peer group when whites mentally bred our nation to exist without a racial nucleus.

Ethically and morally, the task of developing a racial core or a starting point for American Slaves really belongs to white America. That's the first thing they should have done at the close of the Civil War.

To cut all the way to the chase, it's no secret that whites orchestrated our initial lack of core identity. However, what most don't realize is that 'African American' leaders are the ones who are perpetuating our identity crisis and prolonging our lingering ignorance. ❖

CHAPTER 9

The United States Constitution

(It was never intended to cover Slaves)

The U.S. Constitution is firmly established and highly regarded, and rightly so. Unfortunately, it doesn't adequately cover the descendants of American Slaves.

I have talked to whites who believe that all Americans are covered in the Constitution. This is not entirely accurate. Whether they know it or not, their case is diluted with doubletalk. Their argument is directed at individual Americans, not the American Slave *nation*.

American Slaves are discriminated against as an American people, and as a *group*, yet the Constitution doesn't recognize us as an ethnic group, tribe, or a nation. Using hindsight, we recognize that our country's founding fathers didn't have American Slaves in mind when they constructed the Constitution. Slaves were being bred, brutalized, and sold, commercially — *in part by some of our country's founding fathers* — even as the U.S. Constitution was being drawn up.

The Constitution doesn't provide an avenue for descendants of slaves to gain equal status. Impersonating African Americans is not equal status given who we are and what our ethnic group contributed to America.

If descendants of slaves are to achieve equality, we need to be included in the U.S. Constitution, or be given direction in the form of a constitutional plan that shows clearly, step by step, how it will assimilate our people into mainstream America. This diagram must clearly illustrate how the American Slaves will be *fully* included in the American system, and not as immigrants or second-class, disenfranchised people who will continue to be discriminated against and deprived of true freedom. The American Slaves' course must be carefully charted by those who understand ethnicity. Our ultimate goal is to be recognized as the first and only born 'racial group' of America because that's our proper identity and should be our proper position.

Starting from scratch

*B*efore we go any further, allow me to compare the slavery situation in America to a black/white situation I once got involved with. There was this rich, white family. The white husband committed rape and fathered a black child in the ghetto. The child grew up in ignorance and suffered in poverty as she watched her rich parent and her other "half kin" wallow in relative luxury. Everyone knew who the child belonged to and how the child came about but, because of fear and ignorance, no one would talk about this miscarriage of justice. This story reminds me of the descendants of slaves. No one wants to talk about our people either until there is a racial flare-up, and then the talk is always negative.

Fear and shame derived from rape caused the innocent child to be overlooked, to grow up ignorant of who she really was and to forfeit her birthright. This same type of fear and shame has bred an ongoing ignorance among our people.

Compared to the age of other population groups, American Slaves are still in our infancy. Infants are supposed to be cared for by their parents and learn from them, and I'm not talking about in the form of pitiful welfare. If the white race were to mentor American Slaves properly, even the lowest of us would have a chance at achieving the American dream. Proper, parental leadership would also ensure our group of having a

"Slaves were being bred, brutalized and sold, commercially — in part by some of our country's founding fathers! — even as the U.S. Constitution was being drawn up."

smooth transition into becoming a successful people.

Since Dr. King was assassinated, it is clear to see that our arrested mentality has lulled a majority of the descendants of slaves to sleep. The drift toward welfare has caused a majority of us to resign ourselves to remaining silent paupers. This silence allows greedy politicians to unjustly modify slaves' circumstances to benefit themselves, and it allows whites and foreigners to profit through our people and mistreat the weaker of us.

Whites abusing American Slaves is a terrible thing. Whites being in control of America and then allowing other ethnic groups to come into our country and mistreat *America's only offspring,* after their ancestors maliciously programmed our ancestors for servitude because of their greed, is parallel to a father letting outsiders come into his house and abuse his children after he, himself, has abused them. ❖

CHAPTER 10

Man's Best Friend

(Exploring the unknown)

Some who oppose American Slaves becoming a recognized people might say American Slaves *are* included in the Constitution. Others will say that we are not the only offspring of America; that every child of immigrant parents residing in America is bred in and born to America and therefore, included in the American Constitution.

That's not my argument. I'm not arguing for individuals. I'm arguing that American Slaves, *as a people*, are not included in the Constitution; that we are the only *race, nation, ethnic group*, or *community of humans*, to have been bred in and born to America. We are a *distinct population* group that was deliberately and forcibly bred to serve whites, using crueler methods than applied to barnyard livestock.

Let us put cruelty aside and look at human life in a broader, more down-to-earth sense, *psychologically*. American Slaves being a present day

"We must keep in mind that not only did whites train our foreparents to give them a mindset that would accept slavery; our progenitors were also selectively bred, physically, so they could be recognized as slaves."

reality, is the opposite of what Americans have been taught to think, believe, and accept.

Just as individuals are born, breeds of people are born, also. How else did the world wind up with so many different nationalities? Could it be that, because of the way American Slaves were conceived, the founding fathers were ignorant of the fact they were conjuring up a new human breed?

Up to now, we have been dealing mostly with the slave mentality that was forced upon our people because our racial mentality, or slave outlook, is what controls our people *emotionally*. Our leaders having slave mentalities is what allows other nationalities to take advantage of our group. Ordinary slaves having slave mentalities is what allows individuals from other ethnic groups to take advantage of descendants of slaves, individually.

It was necessary to the success of slavery that slaves' be 'mentally bred.' It's the only way they would acclimate to slavery. Americans have always looked at slavery as a physical condition that was reinforced with chains, whips, and other abusive measures. However, slavery is also a state of mind.

Let's follow the trail of slavery up to now and study racial discrimination with an open mind. The first thing we realize is that it has always been our looks, or our appearance which allows us to be easily recognized and, consequently, discriminated against. It was always intended for our people to be dark skinned so whites could distinguish between slave and master. But the slave masters injected their blood into our being, causing descendants of slaves to wind up with a different, multicolored, physical appearance. We must keep in mind that, not only did whites train our foreparents to give them a mindset to accept slavery, our progenitors were also selectively bred physically so they could be recognized as slaves.

Individual immigrant families, other than captured slave chattel, have always been free to mate with whomever they choose, or even choose not to have offspring. American Slaves were forcibly crossbred and inbred with specific goals in mind. Slave masters chose breeding partners — sometimes even white studs (themselves included) — in order to improve power and endurance. They then used mind manipulation and brute force to reduce the traits of independence and assertiveness in their chattel even their own progeny if those offspring were slaves.

> *"Through selective breeding and mind manipulation, whites could premeditatedly control how their slaves looked, and, at the same time, control how slaves behaved, by taking away their ability to properly conceptualize their true being and then classifying them as animals."*

Deliberate restraints on the information necessary to think logically according to their surroundings and who they were in comparison to others, allowed the master to reduce his slaves' status to that of animals. Through selective breeding and mind manipulation, whites could premeditatedly control how their slaves looked and, at the same time, control how slaves behaved by taking away their ability to properly conceptualize their true being, and then classifying them as animals.

With "selective breeding" in mind, let us compare animal reproduction as a parallel to prove our point that American Slaves were made into a new people. In this case, we will use a well known species of dog because American Slaves, like some dogs, were bred from mixed stock on American soil.

We all know there are more mixed breeds of dogs in American homes than there are purebreds. Similarly, the average American citizen is a mixture of bloodlines. There is no such thing as a purebred race of people anywhere in the world, much less in this "melting pot" nation of ours. Asked what breed a pet mutt is, many owners might blurt "just All-American dog." On the other hand, a well-defined, easily recognized breed is the Doberman pinscher — hardly a prehistoric species, but uniquely a product of the latter half of the 19th century. It, too, was selectively bred from mixed stock.

The Doberman's ancestry includes the old German Shepherd and the German Pinscher. With obvious lineage of Rottweiler and greyhound, there are also traces of terrier and Weimaraner. Despite this hodgepodge of ancestry, through selective breeding the Doberman has become accepted as a new breed, in and of itself, recognized as distinct the world around. Out of a mixture of crossbreeds, a formidable breed was born. It is now accepted as unique, though its origins are murky.

The American Slaves, as an ethnic group, or as a nation, had a conception which parallels that of the Doberman. Regardless of our ancestry, our breed's origin was *in America*. Though infused with various bloodlines, we remain a recognizable group of people bred in and born to America. No one suggests the Doberman should, or even could, "go back where it came from" because it couldn't and neither can the American Slaves. The slaves of old were disconnected from the way they thought, what they knew, and what they could remember before slavery, at the roots.

The Doberman was accepted as a species of dog and then given equal status to that of other dogs competing in the animal kingdom, as dogs. After it was accepted, it was then recognized for its superior, distinctive traits. The Doberman now stands tall and proud among the elite dogs of the world. Once our origin is defined and we are recognized and accepted and given a fair chance, American Slaves will stand tall among the other populations that compete in the human race and in the American economy.

"Regardless of our ancestry, our breed's origin was in America. Though infused with various bloodlines, we remain a recognizable group of people bred in and born to America. No one suggests that the Doberman should, or even could "go back where it came from" because they know it couldn't. Neither can the American Slaves."

The contents of this book are intended to help the descendants of America Slaves recognize their heritage, to acknowledge their true origins, and to embrace their essence. We are not African Americans any more than the so-called "sons and daughters of the American Revolution" are English Americans or Scottish Americans. Descendants of slaves are not Africans who have become African Americans — we are 'Americans' bred from slave stock — hence, *American Slaves*. Even though our slave nation contains the blood of many nationalities, we have always been in America. Our common heritage was conceived right here! ❖

CHAPTER 11

Thinking Can Be Contagious

(Who thinks for the descendants of slaves?)

No matter what slaves are called, since their inception the mentality of American Slaves has been deprived of effective, internal leadership. Rational thinking is something we, as a people, have not had a lot of experience with, and we haven't had any experience with commercial thinking. Now, ask yourself: In an industrialized country, how can descendants of slaves be truly free if our group can't even think for themselves? How can we function as a team if the leadership cannot understand who we are, or even perceive that we are a unique group?

Whites shouldn't jump to conclusions, and the descendants of slaves shouldn't be ashamed because people who look like themselves are thought to be defective because of the way we talk, think, and misbehave, especially toward our own kind. American Slaves are not substandard; we just are not fully developed yet.

> "Slaves must accept the fact that, since slavery, we have had an identity crisis. We must now deal with the fact that our roots are entrenched in slavery. It's important that we realize we cannot "go back to Africa."

Slaves must accept the fact that, since slavery, we have had an identity crisis. We must now deal with the fact that our roots are entrenched in slavery. It's important that we realize we cannot "go back to Africa." As a people, we have never been to Africa. I stress this point because we cannot proceed on our journey to freedom until *after* we accept our identity and recognize our true being. Organizing ourselves, and going on record as who we actually are, is the only way we can become a legitimate, documented people. America cannot, and will not, recognize us until we take these steps. If we decide not to take these steps our true identity will remain abandoned which, no doubt, would please the now deceased slave masters because we would have played right into their hands.

To be properly organized, we must choose one leader to lead all of us — one who understands who he is and who we are. Only then can we move forward as a group. Right now, our leaders are confused; they choose themselves. Therefore, their little cliques move forward, leaving the bulk of slaves behind to become welfare statistics.

Proper thinking is the only force that can head American Slaves in the direction of true freedom. Once we are collectively formed, maintaining proper leadership will be the main avenue used by our people to keep freedom working smoothly. Therefore, our best leaders, white and black, must come forward.

Why not Civil Rights groups?

Civil rights groups are revered, and sometimes rightfully so. However, the descendants of slaves need to understand clearly that these groups are *not* leading us. Civil rights groups have never represented our people, as a whole, nor should they ever be allowed to. A leader chosen through the electoral process should represent the descendants of American Slaves.

When slaves were released, those slaves who became leaders

"We cannot 'go back to Africa.' As a people, we have never been to Africa."

were unaware juveniles compared to mature white leaders. Slaves hadn't been taught to be leaders of people. Slaves were bred for strength and endurance, and trained to serve and follow white folk.

Ignorant Uncle Toms wound up leading a bunch of ragged slaves who had been discarded. They didn't know that the people they were leading were due recompense from the country that enslaved them. Slaves were still trying to get the hang of just being regarded as human.

It never occurred to the slaves that the North and South were fighting over organized power. Had they been able to think like leaders, they would have known that, in a commercialized society, adversaries never organize outsiders to compete against them for their power. Organizing slaves was the last thing the North had in mind.

Being unable to compete, and deprived of the basic foundation of knowledge needed to think logically in a commercial society, the American Slaves found themselves abandoned, and our people have never advanced past this doomed-to-failure stage. We are still languishing in the same spot, except for the few individuals who fortuitously stumbled upon logical thinking, glimpsed a bit of direction, and escaped the fate of most. The masters of the game went about their business, and those of us who found a way to escape did. Most American Slaves were, and are still, left out in the cold.

The Civil War and abolition made the white slave owners turn their slaves loose, but the crimes of slavery were already committed. The damage was already done and the wealth was already accumulated — at slaves' expense. Until this day, no one has made white America, the slavery perpetrators, nor their descendants, accept their inherited responsibility and pay for the damage that was done to American Slaves.

In America, when a debt is owed, it doesn't go away just because the injured party doesn't sit on your doorstep waiting to get paid. Interest doesn't stop accumulating because pressure is not directly applied, or felt. If a crime is committed today, the police will enforce the law, but it's up to the injured party to file charges for restitution in a civil court. They then must litigate those charges. This is what should have happened after the Civil War but, for obvious reasons, no formal charges were filed. Slaves were clearly the innocent victims of slavery, but they were ignorant and, to an unfortunate degree, still are.

Because of this ignorance, our racial group has never been properly represented by the law, or according *to* the law. There cannot be a "statute of limitations" on the crime of slavery in America because the injury could be everlasting.

The original slaves knew they were not supposed to exercise judgment; thinking was the master's job. Being wrongfully forced out of slavery, destitute, and then having to go through hell during the civil rights movement, some of our people should have learned something about rational conceptualization. Those of us who are businesspersons have had to deal with sometimes unscrupulous whites in business. I know I have, and it forced me to think. I admit it was difficult at first because I didn't know where to start, or how to *properly* focus my underdeveloped brainpower.

To make a long story short, with the help of those whites who were taking advantage of me, I finally got the hang of thinking for myself, and then I applied it to human evolution. I don't believe I am alone in the 'racial thinking' department when it comes to the development of our people. I believe there are other descendants of slaves out there who can reason in this vein, also. We must come together. Our people need us — *the offspring of our group are evolving in ignorance!* We must think of a way to obtain an authentic leader to guide our people.

What's a leader to do or not to do?

Our leader's job will be to show the way for all of us — *together*. He or she will also take the lead in teaching the masses of us how to think properly. The trickle down from such proper train of thought will improve our overall position in America. I don't believe whites will oppose this improvement of our awareness. Astute whites will understand that our people being properly structured, and then taught to properly conceptualize, will ultimately strengthen America. A business mind knows that strong, prudent leadership is a must, especially when descendants of slaves start dealing with delicate race relations in the coldhearted, industrial arena.

American Slaves have always assumed that civil rights organizations were supposed to think for us, but that's not true. Instead of actually thinking for American Slaves, these businesses mostly consider what others are doing to their small African American cliques. They have shown by their actions they think personal skirmishes are racial issues. These leaders exhaust their energies and use up their resources and power getting whatever media mileage they can from whatever cause is available. They then use up their funds, or budget, paying their own hefty salaries.

Some African American leaders travel to foreign countries that are sometimes in open conflict with America. They claim they are trying to free groups of people who are already free, while leaving our fight unfought. This gesture sends a confusing, negative signal not only to unaware slaves, but to whites within our system concerning the loyalty of our people to our own country. African American leaders' misdirection only makes things worse for the average slave because these guys usually get hailed by their uninformed following as being conquering heroes. Instead, they should be condemned for deserting their own people.

Thinking is serious business to knowledgeable Americans, white and black. We should not allow just anyone to think for the masses and plan for America having a successful future. This is why we hold presidential elections every four years and many local elections even more often.

If African Americans wish to lead the American Slave nation, they must first unite so they can bring our people together. Then they must create one leader-in-chief in order that descendants of slaves can speak with one united voice. Only then can the voice of the American Slaves be heard and clearly understood. It's difficult for our government to understand our needs. African American leaders are all talking at the same time about different things that have no bearing on slaves, or slavery.

The source of inadequate leadership

*B*efore, during, and since our integration battle, help programs, charities, coalitions, and colored folks' organizations

"African American leaders are all talking at the same time, about different things that have no bearing on slaves, or slavery."

have sprung up everywhere. Slaves assumed these organizations were supposed to think for us, fight for our rights, and be responsible for advancing our section of the American population.

From what I can see, the leaders of these organizations are only capable of thinking ordinary expedient thoughts. They are often tricked into fighting for the wrong cause, or for others' rights. They appear oblivious to the very existence of American Slaves, as a distinct group.

Being a young, new entry into the human race, American Slaves are 'newborn.' We are not wide awake yet. Due to the misplaced shame that has always plagued us, there won't be a battery of qualified candidates seeking to lead our slave nation because, as of yet, there is no pride in leading slaves. Therefore, our first leader must be sought out and, if necessary, drafted. We can't let the difficulty of finding a proper leader stop us from seeking one. As our people become successful, potential leaders would then have to compete for the leadership of our group.

American Slaves need one leader to direct the other leaders. He must be an exceptional thinker who will deviate from the norm and from thinking for the moment only. Common sense suggests that, to lead a group of ignorant, abandoned slaves out of degradation, the leader would have to be able to think above-average thoughts.

The first thing our new leader must do is understand the full scope of who we are, and then be willing to teach us how to build on who we are. He must be able to look down the road and see what is needed to bind us together to make us better. He must be willing to go the distance and, if necessary, make the supreme or ultimate sacrifice for his people.

These guys we see on TV, speaking eloquently, are not necessarily leaders. Cleverly formulated catch phrases without substance would signify a weak, "wanna-be" leader. A real leader is a person who knows his identity, his follower's identity, his destination, his route, and be able to communicate a 'collective advancement plan' to those he is leading. Why else would the people follow him?

A great leader is willing to be held accountable for his actions and every word that comes out of his mouth. Now this is important and we must keep it in mind, racial shame is a very powerful force. I know, because I have wrestled with it and, fortunately, I won. Yes, I conquered racial shame, and it wasn't that long ago. This tells me our new leader just might be a fresh, new convert, also. By this I mean he could have just now accepted his slave identity, even as recent as reading this book. That doesn't matter at all, so long as he is *truly converted*.

Openly acknowledging our true being is new for all slaves and learning to accept us *for who we are* — descendants of American Slaves — will be new to white Americans, too.

Why not Human Rights organizations?

Well, that's possible. Our new leader could come from one of these organizations, but first, let's check out their mission statement. Civil rights groups are supposed to protect basic rights and freedoms to which all human beings are entitled. Typically, this includes the right to life and liberty, freedom of thought and expression, and equality before the law.

These groups might do all of that stuff for others, but they have yet to present to American Slaves a racial advancement plan for our approval, also, us being descendants of slaves and never being compensated for slavery proves that equality before the law, for our people, is nothing more than a mockery. Nevertheless, slaves support these organizations and look to them for leadership. Realizing this deficiency, I started nosing around. I wanted to know how these groups could stay in existence and never accomplish anything tangible for our people, the descendants of American Slaves. Well, I found out why — these groups aren't in place to help us. These are businesses. They exist because of perpetual donations, not because of the quality of their leaders' thoughts, dedication to purpose, or loyalty to their following. These guys scarcely know who we are. They don't know that descendants of slaves need a development plan *and, seemingly, they don't care.*

Funds that are donated to these organizations do not go toward the advancement of the descendants of American Slaves. Some of these funds might be used to help get specified slaves out of minor trouble, or to file complaints for individuals whose civil rights have been violated. However, according to what Dr. King said, our next battle is supposed to be fought on the economic battlefield on behalf of all of our people, not in an insignificant, local venue for a few individuals.

When considering an advancement plan for the descendants of slaves, we shouldn't even consider soliciting more welfare, or petitioning for funds to keep failing neighborhood programs ongoing, nor should we seek funds to prolong the existence of civil rights groups. In a modern technological setting, the ultimate goal of American Slaves' racial advancement plan should be to create avenues so that slave business leaders can generate money for our masses — not so civil rights groups can keep begging money for individuals.

America is our motherland and, as such, she should think of a racial business plan, or development plan, for American Slaves as parallel to parents planning for a youngster's future. It's really the same thing, just on a larger scale. For American Slaves to even have a chance at achieving the American dream, advancement avenues must be made available to all of our people, not just Uncle Toms. The cream of the crop will still rise to the top, only faster, *but we will be connected*. If we are joined together and standing as one, no one will get left behind, not even Uncle Toms.

Leadership, where art thou?

Some who read this book could say that I am hardcore, or that I am racist. They may not understand the urgency of American Slaves' situation. I am not hardcore, but since I found my true identity, I am intensely loyal to my being.

As we construct our slavery communication channel, keep in mind that we must elect a leader who will be faithful to slave descendants' well-being first. Instead of thinking for us, many of our African American leaders have become individual profiteers; they fend only for themselves, which is the same as stealing from their people. After they were received into corporate America, acceptance caused them to forget about those they are supposed to be leading. They started behaving like many whites and immediately started seeking wealth above and beyond their needs. Our new leader must not accumulate excessive wealth while leaving our people in bondage.

Whoever is worthy enough to win the right to lead the American Slave nation must first understand that profits derived from our new leader's ideas should not go into his or her pocket, but toward strengthening our ethnic group. In turn, we should reward our leader or pay him or her according to the profitability of their guidance.

Some slaves may not understand this scenario. They may wonder, why should I pay someone to think for me and lead me? I pay for my leadership when I pay my taxes, and I choose my leader at the polls. Slaves must understand — that is legislative leadership. We are a new species of humans; we need racial or tribal leadership that is not ashamed of us. We need a strong, tough-minded leader who is fully race conscious who is not afraid to address our initiation and who has the intelligence to devise a plan that will address our evolving needs.

> *"For American Slaves to even have a chance at achieving the American dream — advancement avenues must be made available to all of our people, not just Uncle Toms. "*

Monies paid to someone to lead our people out of poverty would be a sound investment in ourselves that would pay off handsomely once our new leader gets our division of the American population up and running. If our leader does his job correctly, it's our people who will benefit financially from his thoughts.

To ensure our new leader's salary, the elite of our group should make the initial investment. Those slaves who got lucky in sports, movies, or whatever, or who understand 'financial leverage' and have mastered the fine art of accumulating wealth, should first get their heads together. We should create a pot of wealth that would sustain our new leader through the hard times, or until our sector become stable.

In due course, leaders who are good thinkers, and the financiers who believe in our heritage and who invest in our racial ability, will be more than adequately compensated. These elite would be the 'old money' people in our group; they can be the foundation on which our group builds its financial wealth. If our ethnic group were not profitable, or if we didn't reach a certain point within the allotted or agreed upon time, our leader's pay would cease.

Maybe we can't fire inadequate leaders for not doing their jobs, but if they were elected, we would have the power to impeach them or not vote them back into office again as our leaders.

Using the democratic process, the descendants of slaves could elect a leader of our choice. This would stop shyster leaders from taking advantage of us, and selling us out, while we are unable to do anything about it.

We American Slaves haven't pooled our collective resources; therefore, we have never had group wealth we could use as leverage to get things done for our people. Our group has never even thought about paying someone from within our midst to think for us all. Those who take credit for thinking for us won't think, or don't know it's their job. Slaves who can think soundly usually pursue personal business ventures and, consequentially, reason for themselves only. Like ordinary slaves, they suppose civil rights organizations are representing our ethnic group. It follows that the leaders of our nation are stuck in a ruinous, nonthinking mode. Some of us must start working selflessly for our people.

Slaves who become leaders must learn to cooperate with each other; they must master the art of creating concepts *collectively*. Then they must be able to put the plan into writing, so that it makes sense to America because our mother country is who we must sell the plan to.

But ultimately, and most important, if America won't accept us as her only child, it will be vitally important that we accept ourselves for whom we are. We must never give up. To continue our existence, and then excel, it is important that our leaders learn how to physically move themselves and our people in the direction of *whatever* racial plan we come up with without struggling against each other. If we could ever learn that we are all on the same team, change is inevitable and progress will be quickly identifiable.

The mentality of the original slaves was diluted with shame. To overcome this negative condition, the American Slaves' plan must be constructed around pride, not pity; pride in who we are, and pride in knowing that descendants of slaves now have avenues available to them which will help them excel in American life. Only then will a real slave have reason to take pride in America. There is no pride in belonging to a family that continually mistreats the offspring. In comparison, there is no pride in belonging to a country that enslaved our foreparents and now discriminates against our people.

Our plan can be humanitarian in scope, but it must be business-oriented and carried out with military precision because that's how America operates. If our plan is not approached in a businesslike manner and is not executed in a commercial, businesslike way, it won't work. This would be a tragedy because it would ruin our chance of being truly free.

We must understand up front that for slaves to be included in the U.S. Constitution, it's going to take careful planning, racially. To be included in the American socioeconomic mainstream, it will take precise execution, commercially. It would be unforgivable for our leaders to be too proud, too embarrassed, or too ashamed to learn how to think ethnically so they can figure out our proper position in the American structure. There is no shame in American Slaves being ignorant; it's not our fault. However, there is shame in us remaining ignorant *in the midst of intelligence*. Ignorance is common and widespread among human beings. That's why there is a process called learning. ❖

CHAPTER 12

Where Is Thy Pride?

(A close look at racial shame)

The shame of slavery is a shunned topic in America, but it is still real. Whites are the true heirs of the shame surrounding slavery and should be made to carry this burden. However, when we look closely at slavery, we see that whites programmed their slaves to carry 'weight' they didn't want to bear. Slaves picked up the shame of slavery and have been carrying it for whites, during and since slavery.

> *"Slaves picked up the shame of slavery and have been carrying it for whites, during and since slavery."*

Only through our own efforts will we unburden ourselves of the shame of slavery that still shackles our nation. It is a heavy burden that has not gone away automatically and is now hampering our evolution.

I have always known about slavery and, offhandedly, I was told that my ancestors were slaves. However, because of the systematic way America has tried to cover up slavery by removing it from sight and now gradually from memory, and because the average slave can't think past what he hears, I had never really thought in-depth about slavery. I definitely didn't think of myself as actually being a slave. I casually accepted slavery as a bad thing that happened to some help-less, innocent, dark-skinned people in America long ago — so long ago and so very far removed that I never felt anything personally. That's about as far as most slave descendants' thinking goes regarding our ethnic identity and our racial history. The average slave feels the nagging oppression of slavery, but we don't understand what we are feeling; we just know that it's uncomfortable. It's common to hear a descendant of slaves say he is a slave, but this is mostly an expression of discontentment. The average slave doesn't feel any real attachment to slavery.

Most descendants of slaves hear about race and racial incidents continually. It was only lately that I came to really understand "race" as it relates to the many ethnic groups that reside in America. To my way of thinking, in regard to humanity, there is only one race on earth — *the human race*. Even though descendants of slaves are treated differently, I never thought I had a genuine ethnic history. Most descendants of slaves fully realize they are discriminated against but, because of the missing chapters of slavery, we don't connect our being discriminated against to slavery, or to our people being slaves. I admit I never wanted to be connected to slavery because I have always been instinctively ashamed of it. I now realize the shame of slavery is why not too many people, including our leaders, both black and white, are openly discussing it.

It's reasonable to assume that our ancestors were ashamed to be slaves. However, when we look back, it is clear to see that the white slave masters were not ashamed of themselves for initiating slavery because, at that time, slavery was a most profitable business. Whites took pride in slavery and in what their slaves produced. Some of their best times were spent at the slave market, buying, selling, and comparing their valuable slaves.

Pride in America was passed on to whites, but our ancestors didn't take pride in slavery, and they definitely didn't take pride in America for making them into slaves.

"Whites took pride in slavery and in what their slaves produced. Some of their best times were spent at the slave market, buying, selling and comparing their valuable slaves."

Therefore, our ancestors didn't have any "American pride" to pass on to the descendants of slaves. Whites *inherited* American pride, but American Slaves did not. It is my opinion that whites don't know this because it's a good bet that African American leaders haven't even considered it. If they have, it's safe to say they haven't relayed this information to whites because no Uncle Tom has the intelligence, or nerve, to tell whites in upper positions he is not proud of America. Love America, yes; proud of America, no.

Knowledgeable slaves would never say they are proud of America, knowing what America did to our foreparents and what it is still doing to our people. Only an Uncle Tom would say he is proud of America, knowing that America hasn't seen fit to do anything about slavery.

To sum up: American Slaves are not recognized because slavery is being covered up. Slavery is being covered up because of white shame.

It falls to our leaders to explore this shame. Once they understand this damaging disgrace, it falls to them to teach us about pride as opposed to shame. To do that, they must teach us who we really are — *that will expose our unwarranted shame*.

Our leaders must reinstill pride into our being. That won't be easy because during slavery, whites created a myth that American Slaves were inferior to other human beings. This tells us that even then whites knew they had held back our groups' normal, mental growth.

It wasn't until I realized my true identity that I understood slaves are not, and never were, substandard, unless we consider abused people inferior to those who committed the abuse.

Racial pride in my life has brought forth a strength that I never knew I had. Pride in who we are *racially* is all around us. It's right before our faces, but being submerged in ignorance. Slaves don't recognize it because we don't recognize we are slaves. Not recognizing our true being, we wouldn't understand racial pride, or racial love, in regard to ourselves.

Since I found out who I am, racially, I take pride in who I am. I feel special being an American Slave because, when you think about it, we are special.

Family pride

*M*y parents often said: "My darling son, always take pride in yourself. And, if you want to better yourself, don't forget to pray, and always seek the truth — because the truth will set you free!" Well, I was obedient; I took pride in myself, and now I am proud of my *true self*. I sought the truth and I stumbled upon my identity. I didn't forget to pray — and it did set me free. But it's an individual freedom; it's one-sided. In my search, I also found out no one person can be truly free until his people are also free. The way I figure it, individual American Slaves who think they are free aren't completely free — they're merely escapees. During corporal slavery they would have been called runaways.

Racial Pride

When we look closely at 'race,' as the term is perceived by most Americans, we see that white Americans and American Slaves were entwined during slavery. We are family — whites are the parent race; America is the mother country and descendants of slaves are the offspring culture. Nonetheless, there has never been any racial guidance, family love, or any other kind of love generated between our two people. Neither group takes pride in our two people being entwined, only shame and hate.

"Since I found out who I am, racially, I take pride in my being — I feel special being an American Slave because, when you think about it, we are special. "

Whites created our slave mentality, and some white slave masters choose to inject their blood into our being. Because of this transgression, our two people can never be separated. Yet, if discrimination continues, we will never live in peace together. America and white Americans are glorified. American Slaves are being largely ignored, and that's just wrong. Inherited shame causes our contribution to the building of America to be maliciously downplayed, or simply overlooked altogether.

It's the lack of communication among descendants of slaves that causes our people to bear white shame. Black leaders do not communicate with those of us who have ideas that could help our people. They feel threatened because we are aggressive when it comes to our people. Ignorance causes them to fear another slave being in the same arena with them. They think we would be competing for their Uncle Tom status, causing them to lose their position. If they recognized their true being, they would realize we are trying to lend a helping hand to our culture. A true leader would know that a real American Slave who knows who he is would never vie for Uncle Tom status, but we sure could use some of those high-up positions our Uncle Toms are wasting. Some of us common slaves who have operated in the industrial arena would know how to finish freeing our people wielding that kind of power and having those kinds of connections.

Don't blame me

When we get at the root of misplaced shame, we realize descendants of slaves, being unconsciously ashamed of slavery, also makes us ashamed of our foreparents for being slaves. Therefore, we are instinctively ashamed of ourselves for being descended from slaves. This tells me that racial shame and unconscious revulsion for America was passed on to the descendants of American Slaves — not American pride. America is compounding covered-up disgrace by not dealing with the aftereffects; yet, it's the only way we can properly correct and rid ourselves of the defect.

Leaders can't pass pride on to their followers if they themselves don't have any. African American leaders should understand that the American Slave nation could never be proud of America until the stain of slavery is removed from the fabric of America, and the subconscious pain from years of denial and abuse is dealt with to our people's satisfaction. The only way slavery can be properly dealt with is through exposure.

If our leaders were proud of their real being, they would have accepted their true identity. They would have planted the seeds of pride and hope in our people long ago. They

---

"Descendants of slaves being unconsciously ashamed of slavery also makes us ashamed of our foreparents for being slaves; therefore, we are instinctively ashamed of ourselves for being descended from slaves. This tells me that racial shame and unconscious revulsion for America was passed on to the descendants of American Slaves — not American pride."

would have taught all descendants of slaves that, just because we are not truly proud of America, still, we should *openly* take pride in ourselves. I take pride in my ancestors for being strong enough to survive the degradation of slavery. Being a true born American, I will do my part to make America a place that I, too, can someday take pride in.

The very first day I became fully aware of who I was, the burden of 'white shame' I had been involuntarily carrying lifted itself from my shoulders. It was strange, but wonderful, because when shame left, pride took its place. Our ancestors really deserve a lot more recognition than we give them. Instead of praising them when the topic of slavery comes up, we flinchingly deny them with our shameful silence. Upon my awakening, I wanted to tell the entire world how proud I was of my ancestors. I wanted to shout it from the rooftops. I wanted our ancestors to know:

We made it this far — *we still have a chance to make it to freedom!*

Inherited ignorance and our inborn, sympathetic mindset have always caused slaves to be subconsciously ashamed for whites, instead of us being ashamed of whites, but we haven't understood this. However, there are ways to test ourselves to see if we are involuntarily carrying white shame. The next time the topic of slavery comes up in a racially mixed crowd, pay close attention. You will notice that whites don't seem to be affected, but that sinking, sick feeling that leaps into the pit of your stomach is the shame of slavery. The topic of slavery will cause this aftereffect to appear every time. If the topic of slavery doesn't make this affliction appear, the word 'nigger' will certainly get the show on the road! Now, ask yourself why.

There was a time when I thought I was one of the few affected in this way. After talking to other descendants of slaves, I realized I was far from alone. Every one of them admitted to feeling strangely ill, or racially uncomfortable, when the topic of slavery or the word nigger came up in a racially mixed group. They admitted that other topics they discuss with whites never upset them. They couldn't understand why the topic of slavery, or them being called a nigger by whites, affected them in such an adverse way. Well, I'll tell them why — they have forgotten about slavery even though it took place only a short time ago. Chronological events reveal that the gash of slavery was left untreated. A war was fought to end slavery, but no one attended to the wound caused by the enslavement. Racial unrest and the violence it breeds is nothing more than a signal to remind us that slavery *still* needs attention.

Once I understood I am an American Slave, I knew I didn't have to suffer the pangs of slavery the rest of my life. My ancestors have already paid the price. Neither do I have to feel the bile well up inside me from carrying the white shame of slavery. This shame belongs to those in the white race who are blessed with a conscience.

"Chronological events reveal that the gash of slavery was left untreated; a war was fought to end slavery, but no one attended to the wound that was caused by the enslavement.

Racial unrest and the violence that it breeds is nothing more than a signal to remind us that slavery still needs attention."

Today, denial is the favorite tool used by whites to avert white shame regarding slavery. Whenever restitution for slavery is discussed, modern day whites defend their American wealth saying they are proud of America, but in the next breath they say they didn't have anything to do with slavery.

Whites know full well that America produced human slaves, and that's not something a decent person should take pride in. Whites also know we are the descendants of those same slaves who helped build the foundation of America; that's something descendants of slaves can take pride in. Whites admit they are proud of America, but by them not doing their part to rectify slavery they are helping to keep it covered up — *they are sanctioning slavery.* Whites fail to understand that our people, just like America, grew from the seeds their forebears planted. ❖

CHAPTER 13

Anger Control

(Built up anger, wrongful intimidation, dangerous situation)

When slaves start to arduously apply their minds, realization derived from this new, intense approach will cause attitudes to shift, and it's likely hard feelings will surface. It's a good bet that few of the leaders in our country, black or white, will comprehend that this is nothing more than a normal part of the healing process American Slaves must go through during the birth and awakening of our slave nation.

Normal childbirth for individual human beings has always been a painful process, but the pain is usually temporary if the procedure is carried out properly. Since we are now beginning to understand human evolution, I reason that the pain from our nation's birth should also be temporary as long as there are no bigoted complications.

"Bigotry, bred by ignorance, stops whites from realizing that even though our two cultures have an in-house problem that needs to be straightened out, we are all still on the same 'home team' and always will be."

History has been known to repeat itself

The riots across America following the assassination of Dr. King were a sign of what happens when a group of ignorant people are left without adequate, internal leadership. Those riots were only a prelude to our people coming fully awake while submerged in ignorance, and without intelligent guidance.

Any mood shifts caused by slaves waking up, or gaining racial intelligence, must be understood and controlled by slave leaders who have gained some knowledge as to who we are. In fact, mood shifts should be expected, understood, and then planned for. I don't mean with fire hoses and attack dogs, either.

Only those who have the capacity to understand cultural evolution will know that our awakening is not a hindrance to whites or another camouflaged stumbling block put in the way of descendants of slaves but, instead, a timely, positive advancement for our people — *our time has come*. It can be a beautiful awakening, or it can be an ugly nightmare. It depends on the fairness, the intelligence, the skill, and the timeliness of our country's leaders and the learning capacity of slave leaders.

Some whites may not care for American Slaves becoming a functioning entity, gaining in intellect and having racial strength. They might become intimidated and think the descendants of slaves would try to 'get even' for the many evils done against our people. They could even think we would invade or try to take over their white domain. I remind them history has shown slaves are a forgiving people. When we look even closer, we see that slaves were trained to deal with the master's problem only when they were told to, or had to. Slaves weren't bred to "take over." I can't speak for our Uncle Toms, but the accumulation of excessive wealth and power has never been high on the average slave's priority list. Ordinary slaves have never needed the master's wealth nor wanted his problems — *we only want justice.*

Wise team members wouldn't fear the strength of their allies anyway; they would be concerned with the flaws and weaknesses of those on their team. Bigotry, bred by ignorance, prohibits whites from understanding clearly that even though our two cultures have an in-house problem which needs resolving, we are all still on the same 'home team' and always will be. Our two cultures are bound; divorce is not possible, and our abandonment is not working. It is common knowledge our two cultures have their differences. Still we're family — all Americans. Using intelligence, we can work out our difficulties.

"Only those who have the capacity to understand cultural evolution will know that our awakening is not a hindrance to whites or another camouflaged stumbling block put in the way of descendants of slaves, but, instead, a timely, positive advancement for our people — our time has come."

American Slaves wanting to improve their chances at success in pursuit of the American dream, *in their own country*, is not an invasion. Descendants of slaves are not intruders; we're the only begotten children of the abode. We have never had any choice but to reside in a racially-divided country that encourages domestic inconsistencies. This type of controlled bigotry usually breeds across-the-board violence at the worst possible time. It's a good bet that whites don't fully understand the magnitude of this potentially explosive confusion because the descendants of slaves are intentionally stifled.

The American Slave nation is left unattended, and the pressure is slowly but steadily building. We don't have leaders who can look back at slavery and see the cover-up. Therefore, they wouldn't have the capacity to look into the future and see that the festering sore left by slavery could someday erupt.

It is my belief that descendants of slaves who are in leadership positions could report these negative sightings to those who are in positions to correct racial wrongs. But our leaders fear reprisal; they are afraid to report dangers accurately if they think their report will upset whites. Apprehension, plus trying to be political, wouldn't allow slave leaders to unflinchingly tell our country's leaders what lies ahead, even if they could.

Someone must be realistic about all things that could cause racial unrest in our homeland, and they must bring this realism out into the open or to the attention of the powers that be. If they don't, it's the same as one of our leaders having advance knowledge of a terrorist attack, or an all out invasion of our country, and not saying anything until it's too late. Well, it stands to reason if a segment of the people are upset (and they have been continually because of being openly discriminated against) and have nowhere to turn to for help, this is inviting disaster.

Most whites have never taken the time to understand who we are: They look at us but they don't "see us." They see a nuisance. They don't understand the damage their ancestors did to American Slaves during our incubation; they don't even want to hear about it. No matter what we are called when there is a debate concerning American Slaves or their descendents, whites (who are trained debators) make slave leaders (who are not trained deliberators) look like fools. It's not too difficult to make fearful leaders who don't even know

who they are appear to be fools — despite their having legitimate grievances.

There is a proverb that "time heals all wounds" and, while
the slavery wound has hardly healed, it seems those whites who
harbor ill feelings toward American Slaves are confident that
time and ignorance have
served to lessen the impact of
the injury. Discriminatory
whites assume that the time is
long since past for the sleep-
ing giant to "wake up and
smell the coffee" and get all
worked up.

*"Most whites have never
taken the time to
understand us. They look
at us but they don't "see
us." They see a nuisance.
They don't understand
the damage their
ancestors did to
American Slaves during
our incubation; they
don't even want to hear
about it."*

Normally, this would dictate
that instead of the reparations
issue gaining in strength,
momentum is being lost with
each passing day. However, in
my search to establish my
identity, I talked to many
descendants of slaves who are
sincerely concerned about
existing conditions and the
future of our people, and
there are others who, like Malcolm X, seek justice by most any
means necessary.

Keeping the peace

*A*fter hearing the truth, an intelligent person would
rationalize that, according to the age of the American
Slaves community in comparison to other groups in America
and throughout the world, the time is right for our people to
start waking up and flourishing. This suggests that our

country's leaders, both black and white, had better wake up also. Someone must guide us through our early stages of development.

We must celebrate, not alienate

When my eyes first opened to the reality of my being, and I became fully aware of what whites did to my ancestors (and are still doing to my people), I confess, I was upset. However, business taught me long ago that anger stops the flow of intelligent thinking. Business also taught me that concentration and clear thinking will improve communication. However, it was trial and error that taught me proper communication pays off handsomely if the thinker has, and uses, common sense while communicating.

As more information surfaces concerning the aftereffects of slavery, the average slave descendant's eyes will open to the realities of America and we will start to realize who we are and, unflinchingly, face the wrong done to us. There is a possibility that some whites in key positions won't realize how deeply these bad feelings have settled. Because of fear, black leaders act as if they are afraid to inform white leaders of our dissatisfaction, and that's wrong; it's backward thinking. It's withholding vital information, and it is self-defeating.

Slaves in leadership positions are supposed to seize every opportunity to advance their people. They must master the art of dissolving racial anger, using basic negotiations that are beneficial to their group.

I used to wonder why my people seem to stay angry and upset all the time. Well, now I know why. Our frustration stems from us not being able to see past our humble existence. We can't see past our lowly way of life because our true sense of being is missing.

Our leaders are trying to persuade our nation that we are

"I didn't even have the intelligence or take the time to ask these whites what being a minority meant; I was just pleased, proud, and in a hurry to be one. Amazingly, I was the answer to their needs."

African Americans. That makes about as much sense as them trying to convince me that I am a Russian American.

This is how I stumbled upon my identity. I was given a crash course on surviving American business and then, I was thrust into the American business arena. In order for my business to advance, I had to become *a certified minority*. There I was, an undocumented Negro one day, and then an officially certified minority the next day. This prompted some serious thinking about America and me, and the many names my people have been called. Now, all of a sudden — I'm a minority!

Nagging at the back of my mind was — *who am I really?* My uncertainty, coupled with what little I knew about my foreparents being slaves, caused me to think about my being. My thoughts carried me all the way back to the beginning of America to the initiation of slavery. Thinking about me and

America, *in her wholeness*, and that my foreparents were slaves for white Americans, my moral thoughts were: Whites committed a sin that might be unforgivable. My business mentality thoughts were: Still, they have a lot to be proud of. They did a magnificent job building America, but America couldn't have been put together without the help of my ancestors. Thinking about my forebears, morally, and the 'necessity' of them being slaves, commercially, is what adjusted my mindset concerning slavery. I realized that, though compelled under the circumstances of slavery, my ancestors did *one helluva job* helping whites build America. These are the thoughts which settled my mind and brought about my most sobering realization that slavery was just business — a dirty, illegal, immoral business, but nonetheless, still business. It wasn't until after I looked at the whole picture that I was able to accept these hardcore facts without becoming upset. I was actually beginning to understand America. At long last, my anger started slowly dissipating. I understood that being a descendant of slaves could be advantageous because there are tremendous benefits due to American Slaves.

I want to make this clear — even though I am not angry anymore, I still don't agree with making humans into slaves. However, when I look at America, today, *from a business point of view*, I can understand how greed could influence righteous thinking.

Now, let us look at slaves and slavery with the means justifying the end from a moral point of view. According to the laws of morality, it is not considered wrong to father, or "make" children. However, rape is wrong, and it is against American law. If children are begotten because of the rape, whether the rapist is brought to justice or not, it is still against the laws of our land to abuse those children or abandon them before they reach a certain age. Too many times parents abuse and abandon their children, causing them to wind up budding more slowly than other children. This causes us to conclude that American Slaves' abandonment could be considered even more serious than slavery, and just as shameful as the manner in which our mental birth came about *since our racial abandonment and our people's mental subjugation is still ongoing*. It's too late to do anything about our birth; America can't undo the rape. However, our continued abandonment, abuse, and our identity crisis is disgraceful, uncalled for, and must be dealt with to the satisfaction of the victims in order for such disgusting means to justify such a lucrative end!

Even though the fault is not ours, it's still a natural, first emotion that descendants of American Slaves would be upset about slavery and ashamed of who we are. We are the product of the inhumanity that once plagued our homeland. However, once we realize the greatness of who we are, or could become, negative emotional energies that might surface could be properly channeled so the results would be positive. Slaves are really a very special, standout people, and we always have been! Descendants of slaves excel in all areas where whites allow us to participate — *if* the competing is fair.

Survival of the fittest

I have had a long tenure in business. Along the way, I got knocked down many times emotionally. I had to learn how to pick myself up mentally. To survive, I was forced to concentrate on each step that took me from the ghetto of Eddy Alley, to becoming a businessman, to becoming a certified minority, and then to becoming "Minority Manufacturer of the Year." The concentration that went into each transformation allowed me to better understand America. It wasn't until I reached the business arena that I came to understand what really engenders freedom and, also, what guarantees that freedom — it's KPE (knowledge, planning and execution)! ❖

CHAPTER 14

Blatant Lack of Knowledge

(Shame and ignorance working in harmony)

Not understanding how leadership *really* works, descendants of slaves have fallen into the pattern of not expecting our leaders to be real leaders. This is evidenced by our not holding them accountable. 'African American' leadership is a laughing stock among American 'movers and shakers' because it's so hopelessly fragmented and unaccountable to anyone. There is no "one of us leading all of us." Each self-appointed leader purports he is in charge, but doesn't have to report to anyone.

Million Man March Misstep!

Consider this directly quoted material:

"**Organizers:** Minister Louis Farrakhan, leader of the Nation of Islam; Rev. Benjamin Chavis Jr., former executive director of the National Association for the Advancement of Colored People.

"**Event:** Million Man March, a grass-roots mobilization across black religious and class lines; plans are for an assembly 23 blocks long facing the Capitol on Monday.

"**Goals:** Spiritual and social transformation; a 'holy Day of Atonement and reconciliation' for black men, plus a political agenda or 'manifesto' to advance the cause of blacks. Organizers call for marchers to register to vote."

Blunder instills shame into the ignorant

The lack of dealing with factual information caused our ancestors to be unknowing. This unawareness was passed on to us; therefore, most of us are inclined to be unaware of our leaders' failures.

Even though the Million Man March is old news, it should not be forgotten too soon, nor should the failure to accomplish its publicly-stated mission be overlooked. These people had set themselves up as our leaders, and they had ample time to accomplish their mission.

We will use the Million Man March to illustrate the necessity of KPE (knowledge, planning, and execution) when leading, or influencing a group of people because without knowledge, proper planning is not possible. Without proper planning, execution doesn't have a chance to succeed.

Leading up to the march, the TV stations and news media blared what I thought were good tidings; pride filled the air. I reasoned, "Our leaders are *finally* going to get together."

But, at the march, something was wrong; gloominess held center stage. Suddenly, it struck me what was clouding the overall scene. Black men, or male slave descendants, were told they should gather at our nation's capital to atone. My bewilderment caused me to ask myself: Atone for what? When, where, and to whom did we do this wrong? We couldn't have done anything wrong together — we are still a divided people!

I was forced to conclude that our leaders were asking black men to atone because of who we are — descendants of slaves. I realized that's a wrong move. It sent the wrong message to the wrong people.

Once I was able to view the Million Man March in its wholeness, I was aware this whole shebang couldn't help but cause an air of mystery. As a group of people we have always served and obeyed, and now our leaders are telling us we need to *atone?*

How could that be? Upon birth, our dark-skinned forefathers were forcefully turned into slaves, intentionally kept ignorant, and then left that way. There is certainly some atoning to be done, but not by black men. The only thing black men have ever done, as a group, is to accept abuse. That shouldn't be considered wrong because the only other choice we have ever had is to endure additional or worse, abuse.

> *"There is certainly some atoning to be done, but not by black men."*

Asking black men to beg forgiveness for being treated as something less than God intended us to be shows a clear lack of knowledge and an absence of intelligence by these leaders who brought us together. Now, if these leaders had pointed out a legitimate need for American black men to atone, and if we were to ignore valid reasoning or up-to-the-minute intelligence, then it would have been atoning time.

I was one of the first in attendance. After watching the many dark, innocent faces who gathered to atone for being abused, I concluded it was about time to analyze the leadership of our group. We need to know if permanent mental damage was done to male slaves during our incubation into the human race and then passed on to our present leaders.

When we look at this thing closer, we see that, for American Slaves to even consider atonement without reason, is out of order. That's the posture of a group of people who have done something wrong, collectively, or either they are a group of timid, subservient people who are firmly enslaved in submissive ignorance. On further reflection, I reasoned that groups have leaders. If our group did something wrong, it's our leaders who should be atoning because they are the ones who would have led us into doing that which we are being asked to atone for.

The Million Man March would have gotten a more favorable evaluation, and could have been a rousing success, if only the ministers had gathered together the leaders from every black organization taking credit for representing us, and if those thereby assembled were to discuss a plan for racial unity.

The Million Man March didn't change anything, and it didn't influence white leaders one way or the other. Our country's leaders have seen the amount of chaos that can come from a gathering of hostile Negroes. Therefore, they are not interested in, nor would they respond in a positive way to a bunch of disorganized, wanna-be leaders raising a ruckus about nothing and calling themselves racial leaders. White leaders were primarily concerned about mob control in case things got out of hand. As a rule, a leaderless 'mob' doesn't accomplish anything positive for a group of rabble-rousers. All that is needed to get things done for a group is the thinkers who understand 'KPE.'

But I must give credit where credit is due. These guys do deserve recognition for knowing how to put together a march, though if they thought for one minute they achieved their goals and "transformed black males spiritually," or organized the descendants of American Slaves or, for that matter, *organized* anything else they not only fell short of a bull's-eye — they missed the whole target.

Dr. Martin Luther King Jr. was slain by an assassin when he showed notable progress organizing us. There was no rationalization to kill anyone at the Million Man March, no matter who we were. Even a dim-witted assassin would have understood that these leaders weren't advancing our people, this was regression. They told us we needed to be forgiven, instead of telling the abusers they needed our forgiveness.

These ministers would have been looked on with more favor had they outlined the necessary steps we should take to help us forgive whites for the damage they have done to us.

Then we could get on with the healing process. These leaders could have even told us to atone for being incensed at whites in the first place. Even that would have been better than them doing to black males what whites have always done to American Slaves: confusing us, making us feel guilty for what wasn't our fault, and burdening slaves with more white shame. These leaders didn't even have the intelligence to see that shame is the main reason why people atone! Black men, males of the slave nation, don't have cause to feel shame. Whites should bear the shame of slavery. These leaders, and I use the term lightly, should have been asking white males to atone. They had the right idea, but the wrong people.

> "The descendants of slaves don't have cause to feel shame. Whites should bear the shame of slavery."

A minister recited the Willie Lynch letter about a slave owner who almost 300 years ago, devised a plan to help keep black people divided, thus keeping them in bondage. It was moving, but it was obvious none of these leaders knew how to read between Willie's lines. If they had, they would have understood the psychology he suggested using to enslave our people's mentality in perpetual ignorance.

These leaders know that our foreparents weren't allowed to read and write, but it seems as though that's as far as they could think on the subject of unawareness. It is obvious they haven't thought about the result of not knowing how to read and write — *it's called ignorance!*

African American leaders are still unaware of how the ignorance instilled into our progenitors works, and how it is passed from generation to generation. They have no idea of how to help us.

More ignorance

S ome leaders have suggested that the descendants of slaves
should have a separate state "away" from whites. Now, this
is really enigmatic. I thought they meant distance "away," in
miles, because they always said a piece of land of our own — but
that doesn't make sense. They either fail to comprehend what
they are saying, or they should clarify what they are thinking so
their followers can have a clear understanding of what's really
going on.

Being a businessman, I look at the slave descendants'
quandary from an American business perspective. Leaders
throughout the world know that you should never alienate yourself from the power of America. We must learn how to utilize
our closeness to whites to benefit our overall population.

Perhaps, instead of meaning a "separate state," geographically, they were referring to a separate state of affairs, or an upgraded status, or even a new set of circumstances that could lead to
a new outlook on life (all of which are "separate states"), but
they are all *separate states of mind*.

Why would our leaders be trying to get away from whites,
anyway when every ethnic group that has immigrated into
our country is trying to get next to them? Whites control the
wealth of our country. Most ordinary slaves don't understand that ours is a capitalistic society. We don't see the
potential benefits of our people being next to whites, or at
least next in line. Uncle Toms figured this out on a personal basis, long ago. It's unfortunate their slave mentalities
wouldn't allow then to consider they had their people to
think about, too.

Slave leaders keep overlooking reality. American Slaves
have always been here *with* whites. Whites created our racial
mentality and are responsible for our overall appearance.
From my point of view, since we have always been here with

whites and will always be here with them because we have no place else to go (*and this includes Africa*), isn't it about time we started learning how to make the most out of it? Instead of wasting time on foolishness and fantasizing about being Africans, shouldn't we learn to play the hand that whites dealt us? Being the only offspring of *America*, the most pow-

"Our people need a new state of mind — right where we are."

erful country in the world, I'm quite sure if we were to put our heads together we could come up with something better than impersonating people from a third world country that we Americans try to help because of their dire condition.

Again, our leaders are engaging in backward thinking. Could it be they don't understand the word 'state' as it relates to our people? We don't need to be located in a different state, geographically. That could alienate us from our legacy. Our people need a new state of mind — right where we are. It is not our people's proximity to whites that has us in last place. It's the immature state of mind of our leaders that keeps our group in a negative state of affairs.

Individual ignorance vs. leadership ignorance

Those African American politicians who are supposedly our leaders, have demonstrated they aren't necessarily in the game to help the masses of their people. They learn their superiors' jobs so they can get a raise in pay, not so they can improve their own people's standard of living. Their position is nothing more than a job; they are mere employees.

Our government does not sanction, nor does it pay, racial leaders. Politicians who receive government pay, who have been elected to their job, may pass themselves off as also being racial leaders but they are elected to serve the general public as a whole, according to whichever position they are filling. Our government uses our tax dollars to pay them to serve the broad spectrum of our citizenry.

Our government has never appointed us a leader nor has it authorized any of our elected leaders to directly represent us. The United States government knows full well that descendants of slaves are discriminated against throughout *our own country*; yet, no administration has ever even told us that we need a leader to be properly represented.

American Slaves, being ignorant of the inner workings of our government and the importance of having adequate leadership and a plan to follow, allow government employees to stifle us, locally, because they make us believe they are leading us, nationally. This means that, in most cases, our government pays those who we *think* are leading our people. This leaves American Slaves with no internal leadership — except government employees — and our government is largely controlled by whites.

Not knowing the difference between political leadership and racial leadership, our would-be political leaders couldn't begin to understand how to be assertive on behalf of our people in the industrial sector. They parade as politicians, but they demonstrate that they have no idea how to help us in the political arena.

Internal control breeds commercial power

While white business leaders are at the forefront of the white race, our business leaders don't lead our racial group because we don't have any racial backing for our businesses. We don't understand how to help ourselves as a group, or that our group can only be helped through business.

If descendants of American Slaves are struggling in business and require assistance, we can't go to our leaders and ask our own people for help. We must seek help from the white sector through various minority programs. Minority programs are controlled by the white race. They will help us *individually* and, only then, if it's beneficial to the whites who are running the program. Minority programs have the power to certify individuals only, but yet they take credit for helping us as a group.

> **"We are discriminated against throughout our own country!"**

To advance, descendants of slaves must have precise direction in the form of our own specialized program, tailor-made to our needs. To come up with such an exceptional program, our leaders should shed light on our weaknesses as well as recognize our strengths. We must be able to devise a short-term, vigilant plan to start addressing our deficiencies. We need a long-term plan we can all follow to keep us on track and moving forward collectively.

Once we fully appreciate who we are, and actually see our *real* problems in writing, American Slaves will have a better understanding of what is expected of us individually. Seeing our true problems in black and white, and then being given guidance on how to correct these problems, will cause our people to become as motivated as we were during our Civil Rights struggle.

When we realize our true being, see our real situation, and know we have viable leadership and some advancement avenues, we will become unstuck. The day we start truly believing in ourselves and know that we can progress as other ethnic groups have, we will begin to move forward. ❖

CHAPTER 15

Leadership Acquired

(Control and direction)

If African American leaders would be taught to lead like the heads of corporations do, and coach like coaches of professional sports teams, even though we would be starting from scratch, this development would lead our group to function effectively.

It's astonishing that our self-anointed leaders have never figured out our real problems and fashioned us into a united, effectual body. It's also bewildering that these figureheads are allowed to retain leadership positions and not show any proof of acceptable results, and aren't unaccountable to anyone but themselves.

"Our people's leaders don't know how to lead. They still haven't figured out how to get the most for descendants of slaves out of a society that has 'classes' of freedom; our leaders fend largely for themselves."

Those in management, in corporations, and also sports organizations, who don't reach their desired goals using an acceptable plan implemented within a reasonable time, are removed from their positions to keep them from further damaging the plan, or keeping the team or business in a stagnant mode — and this includes the President of the United States of America. Shouldn't American Slaves follow these steps, also? 'African American' leaders are visibly inadequate; yet, they continue to get a free ride at American Slaves' expense.

A group of people should not be considered free until they have adequate leadership, have learned how to help themselves, and are able to rely on the strength of their group for support.

From whence cometh inadequate leaders

*A*merican Slaves have been watching white freedom since our inception, but our leaders have never understood how true freedom for a *group* of people comes about. Just because a person watches a jet airplane fly doesn't mean he knows how to fly one. Just because slaves watch people who are free doesn't mean we know how to be free. We must first be taught the fundamentals of independence through commerce.

As the Civil War was drawing to a close, slaves became even more disoriented. Their only sources of information were the white masters or slaves who parroted what white persons said. Both of these information sources said slaves were freed with the "Emancipation Proclamation." In their unaware condition, slaves had no other choice but to believe what they heard — that they were free. However, American Slaves' freedom has never looked anything like white freedom.

The fact is during slavery the master was also responsible for his slaves' sustenance. After the War, slaves were run off of their master's land without any means of survival. They were immediately set apart and forced into all-out survival competition because they were now responsible for their own support. Newly freed slaves not only had to rival each other for *their* livelihoods, but also had to compete with an intelligent, educated world, including the very masters who had enslaved them.

Soon after the War was over, those slaves who were closest to the master found themselves leading these abandoned people. These chosen-by-happenstance few were submerged in a different kind of ignorance. They worked in the masters' houses. They were always closer to white intelligence than were the field hands; yet, when their time came to lead, they had no foundation to become leaders. Newly freed slaves were too immature mentally to realize they were still locked in the manacles of slavery. They had no conceptualization of our people being a newly bred species being added to humankind. They couldn't have known that our ethnic group was in its formative years, our leaders of today still don't embrace this idea. Our 'leaders' haven't advanced past their mental condition of dependence and servitude. They don't fully understand what is really going on around them in regards to their being leaders of a group of abandoned, destitute people in an industrial setting. Simply put: *Our people's leaders don't know how to lead.* They still haven't figured out how to get the most for descendants of slaves out of a society that has 'classes' of freedom; our leaders fend largely for themselves.

> **"Our leaders must organize and stop competing against each other!"**

As part of reparations, whites owe it to us to properly train our leaders to be genuine leaders while our populace is still young. It will take cooperation from whites, and intense teamwork from all slaves, for our people to flourish.

Our legitimate leaders must come forward. You know who you are!

Those from among our present leaders who have the potential to lead us must organize and stop competing against each other — it's holding all of us back. If ordinary slaves were to see our leaders cooperating with each other and working together for our collective benefit, we would learn to stop opposing each other at the man-on-the-street level.

Racial role model or house nigger?

Many inner-city slaves are reared in single parent families, headed by mothers who work for minimum wage and are dependent on welfare to some degree. As a rule, these struggling women try to set proper examples for their young. Unfortunately, most find it difficult to be appropriate role models because much of their time is spent struggling merely to survive.

Not many ordinary slaves, male or female, have the background, education, or support to be proper role models in our fast-paced, commercialized society. Our role models usually come from individual slaves who find fame in sports or entertainment, or strike it wealthy otherwise. Politicians and other whites in high-level positions use these exceptions at will to give the impression our people are advancing. This is very disingenuous. It programs the unknowing descendants of slaves into thinking that, because of the success of these notable few exceptions, our people must be doing great, or at least progressing.

Gifted descendants of slaves, some whose only attributes are that they can dunk a basketball, catch a football, or knock another person out in the boxing ring, are depicted as black role models by the news media. This is a serious problem because these athletes are gladiators, not leaders. They can't lead because they're caught up in the same identity crisis as the rest of us. They don't even know who their constituency is.

Much of the time, after our elite acquire fame and fortune and pile up the bucks, the simmering shame of slavery shows up. They become embarrassed by those around them. They will use any excuse, except shame, to immediately separate themselves from the suffering of modern day slavery. Instant success sets talented slaves apart. They join ranks with the

"Athletes are gladiators, not leaders. They can't lead because they're caught up in the same identity crisis as the rest of us."

white upper class. Ordinary slaves think of these selected few as role models simply because they observe them associating with upper-class whites.

We have seen many movies about the Civil War and also about slavery. Famous actors who are descended from slaves are often given starring roles in these movies. They act out their parts to perfection. In the motion picture, they get beaten, raped, and maimed; they labor without reward, get thrown into jail on trumped-up charges, and sometimes even hanged or out-and-out murdered. However, for some reason ordinary slaves of today don't make the slavery connection. We don't realize the profundity of the movie. White folk are killing and abusing slaves but, at the same time, *they're fighting to help slaves!*

The movie is about us and who we are as a people. Our true culture is an extension of the cruelty done to our people and the violence that it took to stop this travesty just so we could make it this far. Even though our history is being played out right before our eyes, we don't identify with our people's past. We don't realize those beautiful slaves being abused and portrayed in the movie as slaves are *still* slaves.

Sometimes slaves receive awards for the tremendous job they did acting out their parts in the movie, but ordinary slaves don't link themselves to the facts of the movie. They are looking at the magnificence of their 'leader,' the role model who starred in the movie. It never crosses the average slave's mind that the movie is a lot more than just entertainment. These movies could solve our identity crisis, but there is a problem. Those slaves starring in the movie, as slaves, think they are African Americans. They fail to realize there were no dark-skinned African Americans in America during the era of slavery. To me, such motion pictures are part of a divine intervention to remind us of our identity.

I'd rather be lucky than 'good'

*A*rmed with nothing more than good fortune, well-known slaves, and this includes our brightest stars, conclude they must be exemplary role models, or how else did they achieve so much success?

It is because they are successful *individuals* that they have become *easy prey*. White organizations seek out successful slaves, and slaves who have potential. These agents are often paid to negotiate their contracts, direct their actions, control their newfound wealth, and assist in their upward relocation because they have no racial leaders to guide them and no ethnic group to protect them. It could be said that these slaves have been purchased at 'bargain basement' prices and, as usual, ordinary slaves won't reap any of the benefits. Our true culture won't get any of the credit and, we as a people, won't be recognized or even mentioned. The most damaging aspect of this exploitation of our people is that elder slaves are never given a chance to have input into the outcome of these slaves' newfound wealth, power, and influence.

Talented descendants of slaves unknowingly ingrain their ignorance at the top of our ethnic group. They are often accepted as our role models. Too often they go on to become our leaders. Most of these unaware people are either being paid to preach, compete in the sports arena, entertain, or sell products for corporations.

> *"The most damaging aspect of this exploitation of our people is that elder slaves are never given a chance to have input into the outcome of these slaves' newfound wealth, power and influence."*

Making money in a commercialized society is not a bad thing; it's what individuals are supposed to do. Preaching, doing TV ads, or running a charity is no different, and it would be OK if these portrayals didn't deceive the descendants of American Slaves into thinking all American Slaves are free.

When I was younger, Amos and Andy were portrayed on radio as stereotypical, timorous, sputtering black buffoons. Today, TV doesn't depict blacks as bumbling clowns, but many of our people are portrayed as lowlife drug addicts and criminals, and that's a stereotype as well. The majority of slaves are devoted, upstanding, God-fearing people.

Lately, particularly in sitcoms, we are depicted as living 'high on the hog' and, yes, there are some descendants of slaves who do live as well as they are portrayed, but these are a rare few. Ordinary slaves watch these select few in admiration and awe. The majority of descendants of slaves are poverty stricken or struggling in a perpetual hand-to-mouth existence.

The huge financial gap between the few who made it out of the tenements, and those who didn't, makes ordinary inner-city slaves think they are deficient because the slave who escaped poverty and the slave who didn't were just recently on the same level and, in some cases, close friends. This causes the commoner who got left behind to feel inadequate and have low self-esteem. Each one of us can't be an athlete, movie star, or a gifted genius, but if our gifted few were to fully realize their true heritage and were trained to be suitable role models, they could be a big help to our people because of their status, wealth, and contact with the power structure.

If slaves who have been elevated to a higher status knew how to work together for our people's benefit; if they traditionally came back and helped in a meaningful way, those of us they left behind, we wouldn't have our inherited "crabs in a barrel" mentality (pulling each other back down as we individually try to climb up and out of the ghetto). We could even help each other escape the mental prison most of us live in. Sadly, as it stands, however, once a slave gets free there is scant likelihood he or she will come back and help those left behind. Oh, they think they are "coming back and helping" when they parade through the 'hood showing off their beautiful cars. Sometimes they even stop and talk. Showing off their finery is not helping the descendants of slaves. It just makes the lowest of us feel inadequate. "White acceptance" allowed these few slaves to rise in financial stature and popularity only — not in racial, mental maturity.

Now that I have been racially awakened and know who we are as a people, I see clearly why escaped slaves don't come back and help those they left behind. It's because a short memory, a taste of freedom, and a chance to live in white folks' heaven feels so good, it makes them think everybody is free and able to follow the same path!

Now in defense of those few who have come to realize they are descendants of slaves and might be experiencing guilt for their successful lifestyle in comparison to their people's negative condition, but don't know what to do about it, they should be forgiven. Clearly, if these few were to contribute all of their earthly wealth trying to help their people, they would surely wind up back where they came from. Until there is a strategic plan that outlines how their wealth will help, it won't help, not in the long run, and not without a valid plan that encompasses our entire ethnic group.

> *"If slaves who have been elevated to a higher status knew how to work together for our people's benefit; if they traditionally came back and helped in a meaningful way, those of us they left behind then we wouldn't have our inherited 'crabs in a barrel' mentality (pulling each other back down as we individually try to climb up and out of the ghetto)."*

In retrospect, I am grateful I didn't achieve the wealth I set out to accomplish. If I had, there is no way I would have ever known who I was, or how to come back and help my people because I too was elevated to a higher position. I was living real well in white folks' heaven and my memory was also affected — I thought all slaves were free, too, if I thought about it at all. Fortunately, my transplantation was temporary and I returned to my origin, my American Slave roots. ❖

CHAPTER 16

Going the Distance

(in spite of working against each other)

When I first started in business, my original goal was to become a businessman and make plenty of money after which, I reasoned, I would come back triumphantly and help those I left behind. However, once in the business arena, I was in a whole *new* world — I didn't have time to help anyone else. Like other slaves who are struggling in business, I couldn't even help myself. Without racial backing and the necessary know-how, I was in way over my head — I became easy prey.

To keep my business afloat, it became expedient that I be designated a certified minority. My new role as a minority businessman put me under tremendous pressure. In order to expand my business, I had to hurriedly learn my new position and what responsibilities it carried.

I have always known that

> *"In my effort to help my people, I went to those I thought were our leaders and explained what I wanted to do and how I intended to do it. It didn't take me long to realize that the leaders of our racial group didn't understand commerce. I found out later that they weren't farsighted either."*

whites control America but, because of my lack of involvement at this higher level in the business arena, I had never felt the full impact of unadulterated white control. It became necessary immediately that I learn how to talk and act like a white man would because that's who I was now dealing with. The only way I could do that was follow white men, mimic white men and do what they said. I didn't want my business to fail.

When I achieved a degree of success in the manufacturing arena and was nominated Minority Manufacturer of the Year, I was finally in a position to start doing what I set out to do, *or so I thought*. However, I encountered a detour. I explained to the whites who were training me to mimic their behavior that I wanted to 'give back' to my people. They advised me that non-profit organizations were already in place to supply the assistance I wanted to help provide. They told me I now had a degree of distinction for my success. They advised me that if I wanted to live up to this high honor, my business needed my undivided attention. They said I should do what other minority business-men do when wishing to give back to their community — donate money to charity.

I did take their advice, but I was never satisfied. I wanted to help my people *personally*, I wanted to "feel it," and I wanted to know it was my people who were being helped and what kind of help they were getting.

When I expanded my business staff, I finally found enough time in my schedule to be able to give back to my people with-out it hurting my company, but then I ran into another obsta-cle. I was unmindful of the degree to which slaves work against each other, seemingly for no reason at all. I thought our working against each other was an internal survival mech-anism that lowlife individuals within our racial group misuse for personal gain. I didn't know this was an across-the-board aftereffect from slavery that was instilled into our progenitors to keep our entire population a permanently divided people.

African American leaders think we are together because of our proximity, but that's not true. Slaves have never been *together*. Our people were mentally divided at our inception on American soil.

In my effort to help my people, I went to those I thought were our leaders and explained what I wanted to do and how I intended to do it. It didn't take me long to realize that the leaders of our racial group didn't understand commerce. I found out later that they weren't farsighted either. When they heard I was willing to risk my paltry wealth and my promising company to help my people, they at first thought I was nuts. Then, they thought I must be scheming. They became suspicious because they couldn't comprehend my motives or visualize what I could see clearly: The descendants of American Slaves must start trying to help ourselves. The only way we can do that is to learn to work together — *and some of us must take the first steps!*

> *"I could have spent the rest of my life ... being called an Uncle Tom."*

I explained to these gentlemen that when I went into business I wanted to get rich. I wanted to succeed in the American business arena. However, once in the arena I saw the game was unfair and negatively impacting my people. I told them that I now recognized I had been singled out because I had a special talent which could be beneficial to some scheming whites who were in a position to help our people. However, instead of helping our people, these crooks were diverting our group's racial help to themselves — *and using me to do it!*

I immediately rethought my position and restructured my entire philosophy concerning the white business arena. Ultimately, I rearranged my goals. I was in a strange, uncomfortable position. I was just starting to learn how business is done at the higher level, and it was whites who were teaching me. If circumstances hadn't opened my eyes I could have spent the rest of my life in the American business arena, struggling in racial ignorance and watching my own people suffer because of *my* ignorance. I could have been "as rich as cream," but my people would still be right where I left them, in poverty, struggling in ignorance. They would be calling me an Uncle Tom because these white guys were showing me how to live 'real good.'

When I slowed down long enough to take a real good look at where I had ascended, I realized I was alone. I was now the president of a minority manufacturing company that had great potential, and was on the rise, but I was completely surrounded by 'overprotective' whites. In my feeble effort to help my people, I had been "cut out of the herd." I had actually run off and left my people behind. I could now see why some of those I left behind might be thinking I was an Uncle Tom. This realization caused me to have a sinking feeling, and it wouldn't go away. For the first time in my life, I was beginning to feel and understand racial love.

It dawned on me: I was nothing but a slave in a pinstriped suit. When the right time came and I got the chance, I broke loose and ran away. I made it *almost* to the top of the hill, but when I slowed down and looked back to see if I had gotten away clean I saw what I was running from and I didn't like it. Realization struck home — the Civil War was fought to free me, but I was still running from slavery and that's wrong. That's aiding and abetting the slave masters' plans to cover up the crime of slavery.

It is a fact that when you draw away from a situation, you can see it clearer. A "bird's eye view" gives new perspective. I had been living in my own personal dream world. The picture before me now was real, because it included all of us, white and black, and I didn't care for the deliberate disparity. Instead of my escape resulting in a feeling of elation like I thought it would, it caused me to hurt on the inside. I couldn't stop thinking about my people and how I had failed them. I couldn't forget them. I wanted more than ever to help them — *but how?*

The possibility of my people thinking I was an Uncle Tom was a heavy burden to bear, but the way I figured it I had no other choice. To be perfectly candid, I was right on the one hand but wrong on the other. It was correct for me to accept help from whites in the business arena. Whites owe descendants of slaves the opportunity to participate fully in America *at all levels*. I was still in the right when I mimicked their actions in that arena because who better for me to imitate than the ones who control the game I want to play in. However, this new feeling of *racial love* caused me to look back and analyze correctly. Self-justification and weak excuses are not acceptable, not in the position I was in. Whether I liked it or not — whether I *realized* it or not — I was in a leadership position.

I was in the wrong because I was ignorant. Being a slave businessperson in the same white business arena that enslaved my foreparents, I had an inherited responsibility to my people because slavery was business — *not personal!* However I didn't realize this because I didn't know who I was, racially. I thought I knew it all, but I didn't. I only knew how to do to perfection what these whites taught me to do in order to make the company they had conjured up become successful. I was ignorant of who I was, and it caused me not to recognize my people. My racial ignorance was adding to my people's depression. I was in a leadership position, but I didn't understand how to use that position in the business arena to help my people, rather than use it for my own personal advantage. That's the move of an Uncle Tom who is submerged in ignorance but thinks he's "got it going on." He struts around like a proud Peacock, but he is despised by his people. Like many descendants of slaves I, too, had unknowingly eased into an Uncle Tom position.

The proficiency of ignorance

Slaves who are in business live their lives rubbing elbows with wealthy whites and other people who are in a position to help their business get ahead. Pressure causes them to forget all about their own culture. I am sure other well-intentioned slaves feel right now like I felt then — that once I got my business thriving, I was going to come back and help my people. My intentions were good, but I got sidetracked.

Let me start at the beginning because we need to be aware of cause and effect and how it relates to slave leaders and their followers working against each other. My chief engineer was white, I told him what I intended to do. I also told him the difficulty of helping a group of people who have an *overall* unaware condition. After negotiations, part of his employment package included helping me help my people. We agreed that descendants of slaves would be the first hired and first promoted. Whites would call this reverse discrimination, even though they have always looked out for the well-being of their own group.

Everything went fine until I put the plan into action. The first slave I promoted to manager *turned on me*. He couldn't adjust to taking orders from another slave, and he didn't know why. He became further confused when he saw me giving orders to whites, and their following these orders without hesitation. He started being disrespectful toward his white superiors because he thought something must have been wrong with them for following my orders word for word. Unconsciously, he felt this was not the way it was supposed to be. When we think profoundly about America, we understand, it's an inherited instinct by blacks *and whites* that whites lead. I'm not saying it's right; I don't think it is right. I'm merely saying that's the way it has always been.

When my head engineer saw the confusion and damage we slave descendants do to each other when we try to work together but are ignorant of who we are and, therefore, of what working together entails, his help came to a screeching halt.

I studied the abuse done to me by my own kind. I concluded that slaves are experts in at least one area — we have perfected the art of working against each other. I also learned why black people, in most cases, destroy each other when they do try to work together. It is because of misunderstood shame and hate. Unconsciously, we are ashamed of who we are and we hate the idea we are descended from slaves — *we're slave haters!* So why wouldn't an 'African American' hate a slave who he believes to be in a better position, especially if his rationale told him that, because of his new African American identity and higher education, he belongs there and the slave doesn't?

"Our foreparents, even though they had no other choice, were ashamed of themselves for accepting the abuse of slavery."

Our foreparents, even though they had no other choice, were ashamed of themselves for accepting the abuse of slavery. There wasn't anything they could do about it, so, they hated themselves for being *inadequate* slaves. It follows that descendants of slaves are *inherently* "slave haters." Slave hating is a very *damaging* aftereffect from slavery. We must be made to understand that when we hate slavery, we hate who we are — we hate ourselves — and that's backward.

America needs to understand the descendants of slaves are people who don't love who we are nor the profundity of who we are. That's a dangerous situation and it's still simmering. If we look at America and slavery, chronologically, and then listen to harbingers of an up and coming reparations war, we realize we're just now trying to get a handle on how to "wind slavery down." In a mop-up situation like this, the last thing America needs is a group of people who hate themselves but are trying to negotiate for their freedom against a group of people who don't realize the depth to which they are preju-diced against the negotiators.

Hate in any form is self defeating. The 'brother' that I was try-ing to help simply didn't know his true identity. He was giving in to his presented-at-birth, negative traits. He had no way of knowing that he is supposed to believe in his own kind. If he had known his own identity and understood the plan that was laid out before him, or understood what we could have accom-plished working together, I believe he would have tried to help instead of hate.

My chief engineer wasn't that fond of "coloreds" anyway. He made that more than clear when he resigned. At that time, my entire management team was white, which is how my business rose so fast. My remaining managers called a meeting and made it clear our deal was that I was their leader, that my first duty and my job was leading them, not those who would try to destroy my company. Seems the brother I promoted to manager turned Uncle Tom on me. He got together with those black lead-ers who thought I was nuts and cooked up a hare-brained scheme to take over the company. They talked him into trying to assail my character to my white managers.

Looking back, I recollect it was my ignorance that caused the mayhem in the first place. Being unaware of the inner workings of America, I thought that, because our mayor had put these guys in control of the city's minority program, they were our leaders. However, as it turned out, they weren't leaders at all because they didn't understand how to work together nor did they understand how to work with me, a certified minority. On the other hand, whites do know how to work together — they believe in working together.

To work together, you *must* follow the leader. These guys couldn't comprehend that because I was a 'minority-business-man' I was a leader. All they had to do was get on board and fol-low me. They thought that because the mayor had put them in charge of the minority program's money, they were racial leaders instead of the mayor's flunkies. Ultimately, it was the slave mentality we descendants of slaves inherited that damaged the company because these slaves tried to undercut the slave who was in a leadership position. *That's backwards!* That's how crabs in a barrel work. Apparently, slaves, like crabs, don't know any better — it's our nature.

My remaining managers couldn't understand my being sympathetic toward a person who would try to do harm to an organization I worked so hard at putting together. I told them I held no ill feelings toward him since, like most of our people, he didn't understand business and he didn't understand how to be loyal to superiors, especially if the superior was descended from slaves. I tried to be political when I explained my position. I told them that since my people didn't know any better, it wouldn't be right for me to forsake them when I knew they needed me. Whites know compassion is not a substitute for success especially in business. Therefore, diplomacy didn't help. They also handed in their resignations.

At first, I believed they had their departure planned because it happened so abruptly. However, I heard later that what really upset the 'apple cart' was they concluded, correctly, that I had planned to help my people all along, and not them. The word being spread — I was "simply using my company to help a bunch of darkies who don't want to be helped."

I learned a valuable lesson: Proper leadership is what dictates the outcome of *all* ventures whether it is running a small company, a large corporation, or an ethnic group. Leaders are supposed to have their act together at all times. Business "doesn't suffer fools." It doesn't matter that it was my people I was trying to help or how badly they needed help, business is hardcore, period! And so were my managers when they walked out on me, and likewise our government when I tried to explain what happened. Industry is not set up to tolerate leaders who make avoidable mistakes. Most whites, especially Uncle Toms, think helping the descendants of slaves is not a priority, that it can be avoided. I don't see it that way.

To sum up, when helping my people got in the way of me doing my job, my managers made it clear that struggling to help my people wasn't what my corporation was paying me to do. And they were right according to the company's by-laws.

So, whose job is it to help our people?

Well, at the moment, our central leadership position is open, but whoever gets the job should realize up front that leading the descendants of slaves out of degradation will be a full-time, 24/7, job. African Americans who are looking for a 'moonlighting gig' need not apply.

Once we elect a leader (and are formally organized and our true leader is in position), he must put together a management team. This team of leaders must devise a plan that will entice whites to help us in our endeavors. It's up to our leadership to prove to the establishment by working together that we are not 'crabs in a barrel'; that helping the descendants of American Slaves is a wise investment in America.

Let's get on with it

Now that I understand the ignorance that surrounds all American Slaves *and whites* concerning slavery, I maintain there is hope for us all.

When I reflect back on my "school of hard knocks," I can appreciate what happened, how it happened, and why it happened. I am grateful to those, black and white, who don't understand our situation but are not afraid to speak their mind. The unadulterated truth, even when spoken in anger, taught me a lot. The lesson that I learned is a lot more valuable than the wealth I sacrificed. I gained the much-needed, missing information the descendants of slaves need if we are ever to advance as a people.

Whoever is privileged to lead the American Slaves nation must understand the opposition he will be up against — even from the very people he is trying to help. Being the leader of the American Slaves *nation* calls for a thinking mind, and it's a position for which neither the faint of heart nor the weak of mind need apply. Educating our people properly is going to be a tough job but, someday, someway, someone's got to do it.

> *"This book contains the missing knowledge that our people so desperately need."*

Those who claim they are the leaders of our people, and especially those slaves who are in business, need to be acquainted with problems that hamper our slave nation. This book addresses these problems in open, straightforward, and simple terms. Until the leadership of our people can relate to a parallel, or to something else that is plainly obvious, it's hard for slaves, in our present condition, to relate to the ignorance that surrounds us. When we are 'politically correct,' there is too much doubletalk; too much truth goes unsaid.

Leaders must point out our inherited racial ignorance to each other, and then *collectively* to ordinary slaves. They must learn how to speak with one tongue, and that will take practice, trust, and dedication.

To reduce our racial ignorance, we must bridge the gap between our business leaders and our political leaders. They must start learning to work hand in hand with each other. Then they must create ways to pass on meaningful information — that comes from this new relationship (in simple terms that naive people can understand).

Some descendants of slaves with whom I began my business career are now independently wealthy. I don't believe they knew our racial condition back then because I didn't. According to their actions, they still don't know the ignorance that has a grip on our people even today. They are good businesspersons, *individually*; however, they are still unaware of the power of togetherness. They are lost as to what they should be doing, collectively, about our people's racial condition. They figure their good fortune is a once-in-a-lifetime opportunity *for them only*. The least among us never get a chance to benefit from our successful individuals' learned experiences.

Our present day leaders might not understand that what they are reading at this very moment offers a once-in-a-lifetime opportunity. History suggests that, without due reflection, African American leaders will probably think this is a personal attack, believing I am trying to smear their African reputations. I'm not attacking anyone and I'm not trying to 'blow the whistle' on anyone or "rat them out." What I am attempting to do is cut through the thick cover-up of slavery. Hopefully, I'm not the only one who will come to see what it's doing to our people.

A leader who is sensitive to his people's growing needs should understand that this book contains missing knowledge that our people so desperately need. I am compelled to write it the way I see it. Right now, my job as I see it is to get the information into print and then get it into the hands of those who have the wherewithal and willingness to help spread the word.

Open-minded rationalization

It would be irrational to ask thriving 'African Americans' to sacrifice their accumulated wealth to help the descendants of slaves, but what if they are not African Americans? What if instead, they are American Slaves? In that case, now that some are wealthy, it's about time they gave back to their people in a meaningful way. I am not necessarily talking about their money. In fact, because of ignorance and greed (other than the necessary funds to get our racial plan drafted and our slave nation started on the right track) money could be a hindrance if injected too soon. Until a bona fide, long-term plan is drafted and accepted, we wouldn't know how much money we need, the source of funds, or what to do with it if we had it.

> *"If elite slaves were to openly acknowledge their factual being and profess their true American heritage, the scales of justice would automatically tip in favor of genuine freedom for our people."*

At this point, what we really need from noted descendants of slaves who are thriving is just a simple nod of empathy. If elite slaves were to openly acknowledge their factual being and profess their true American heritage, the scales of justice would automatically tip in favor of genuine freedom for our people. The rest is KPE (acquiring more knowledge, coming up with a feasible plan, and then executing the plan).

Being a businessman I understand that some elite slaves would rather not be on the front lines in the "heat of battle." That's fine as long as influential slaves understand that freedom in America stems from knowledge that leads to collective wealth, *not personal wealth*. Ordinary slaves need an information connection point a lot more than we need money. We need a clearing house all slaves can draw from as a resource. Most of all, descendants of slaves need to know that our elite still care for us, that they haven't deserted us. Just knowing that our elite still care would give us the much needed hope that has heretofore been missing in our group. ❖

CHAPTER 17

Recognizing Retrogressive Civil Rights Leaders

(Distinguishing between earned pride and conventional foolishness)

Knowing how we descendants of slaves feel about slavery, the largest obstacle to true freedom will be the difficulty of bringing our leadership together. Slave leaders don't want to work together because they cannot envision the possibilities in working together. When we follow the trail of slavery up to now, we realize there has never been an advancement plan for our people; there has never been a system through which our leaders *could* work together.

For too long, small splinter groups have caused confusion in and out of our racial group because of their alienation toward the poorest of us and competitiveness with each other. If the leaders of these groups were proper thinkers, they would appreciate the importance of unity. But, as it

> *"Our leaders are the reason we can't get together, and the main reason we are racially confused and always tagging along behind other American groups."*

stands, their divisive mentalities won't allow them to even consider merging because each one of them wants to be the leader.

Being alienated from each other causes these self-
appointed functionaries to become easy prey. Small groups
are more likely to be singled out for persecution or, worse
yet, personally gain from the further abuse of the descendants of slaves. Some, in these factions, may suggest we are
already a cohesive entity because they belong to the same
organizations and attend meetings together regularly. Others
think we are together because they have their annual
forums. Regardless, 'slaves' inherited a legacy of *unconscious*
divisiveness and it's keeping those descendants of slaves,
who think they are our leaders, from gravitating toward one
principal leader. This is another of the lingering aftereffects
of slavery.

These fragmented groups witness major corporations growing
stronger through merger. Slave leaders should realize that if we
would merge into a single force, our collective power (and this
includes our bargaining power) would be greatly and immediately increased, not to mention the factional leader's own individual status.

Using the vote properly

When it comes to internal leadership, American Slaves
have never had any choice in who is leading us. Instead
of staying divided and just following along behind the crowd, it's
time we, ourselves, got our heads together and created some
leadership options. Look at it this way — descendants of slaves
live in a democracy. We can *democratically* choose our destiny
from the best plan and best candidates available.

During our voter registration campaign, insecure whites were
willing to, and did, kill trying to keep the descendants of slaves
from voting. This should remind our leaders how powerful the

vote can be. The American Slaves' vote is crucial to those seeking election to our country's highest office.

Too often what happens is that white politicians who want to get elected to public office seize every chance to court whoever *they think* is our leader. This tells us that if we were structured properly, we could probably control a block of votes that could sway elections. If so, government, at all levels, would become sensitive to the needs of our people. We won the right to vote, but it's obvious that our leaders still don't realize what the victory means.

> *"To use the vote to the benefit of all descendants of slaves, our first step is to use the vote internally to choose our racial leader who would speak for all of us at once — only then would our vote carry weight, externally."*

To use the vote to the benefit of all descendants of slaves, our first step is to use the vote *internally* to choose our racial leader who would speak for all of us at once — only then would our vote carry weight, externally. Not only should black politicians know this — they should make all American Slaves aware of this.

Ever since descendants of slaves have been allowed to vote, we have been optimistic that the vote would be a tool we could use to stop whites from abusing us. The vote, if used correctly, internally, can stop the abuse that our own ignorant, self-appointed leaders are heaping upon all of us.

To attest to our racial confusion, lack of leadership, and blatant alienation (and not knowing what to do about it), let us refer to a couple of items that are currently being played out right here in Louisville, Kentucky:

At 18th and Muhammad Ali Boulevard, under construction is a "Kentucky Center for African American Heritage." Given our present condition, think what the descendants of slaves could have done with that construction money if we used it more wisely. We could have devised an advancement plan that includes all of our people, from all walks of life, and started implementation of it. Similar funding is being wasted on minority programs and 'African American' nonsense all across the country.

If these leaders are truly trying to help us, they are spinning their wheels. A real leader would understand that descendants of slaves need *tangible* help, not monuments and memorials.

Now let us refer to the second item, the headline of *The Courier-Journal*, Kentucky's leading newspaper, dated February 8, 2004. The headline: "One voice, or many?" The subhead: "Growing diversity of views is redefining leadership in the black community."

Five of Louisville's 'black leaders' are featured on the front page of Louisville's leading newspaper. They are photographed in color — and they are looking good. I suppose they are leaders because the article refers to them as such, but it is obvious they are at odds in regards to leadership. After I read the article, I reasoned the headline should have read, "Growing diversity of views is *perpetuating confusion* in the black community." Ask yourself: Where are they leading us to? What is their plan?

Ricky Jones, University of Louisville professor, states, "There is no black political leadership in this city." The Rev. Kevin Cosby, pastor of St. Stephen Baptist Church, the largest 'African American' church in Kentucky, states, "There's not a need for a commander in chief ...There's a need for commitment to change." Cheri Bryant, District 5 Metro Council member, states, "You still need the tree shakers ... people who are unbought, who can speak freely." Junior Bridgeman, businessman, chairman of University of

Louisville board of trustees, states, "Young people today ... aren't looking for one person ruling." The Rev. Louis Coleman, Justice Resource Center director, states, "If you didn't experience the troubles of the '60s, the blatant segregation, you don't really feel the pain."

The above quotes are just a sample of the backward, confused, 'black leadership' in Kentucky; I'm quite sure it's the same all across America. It is obvious our current leadership doesn't have a plan for the future of our people.

"American Slaves must stop these little groups from claiming us, confusing us, dividing us up, and then acting like they don't know why we can't get together."

These people are not our leaders because we haven't chosen them to be so, and, it's not right for them to be passing themselves off as such. Once we become a recognized people and have a true leader there is a possibility these people might take their cue from our cabinet of leaders, of which they very well could become a part of. However, this can happen only if they are chosen and are willing to be team players and, most of all, if they are capable of learning.

American Slaves must stop these little groups from claiming us, confusing us, dividing us up, and then acting like they don't know why we can't get together. Our leaders are the reason we can't get together, and the main reason we are racially confused and always tagging along behind other American groups.

Present day special interest groups do not represent the descendants of slaves because they are not leading us as a group. American Slaves must be able to choose our leader from candidates who make pledges to American Slaves. Those elected should only be reelected when promises are kept. ❖

CHAPTER 18

The 'Root' Connection

(The longest journey)

To more fully understand the slave descendants' condition, I decided to go back to my own roots to inspect the foundation from which I sprang. So, I left 'white folk's heaven' and moved back into my old neighborhood.

Analyzing my old 'hood, I realized this wasn't my racial root, but just a stop along the way. Coming back to Eddy Alley couldn't give me a full, clear picture of my people. Going back to Georgia where I was born wouldn't do it either. To see a clear picture of my *people*, I had to take a mental trip; I had to put my thinking cap on and reflect all the way back to my people's origin. Usually, when slaves think about their 'roots,' it's on a personal basis. It was only after I was past this snag that I was able to reach the tip end of our taproot.

When I was a hell-raising, teenager living in an Eddy alley, I thought being a carousing, carefree Negro was fun, and it was. But finding out who I real-

> "Ordinary slaves must realize: This 'role model' doesn't know how to help us; he just recently escaped poverty, himself. And he probably won't be back anytime soon because no one appreciates being handed a problem that they have no idea how to solve."

ly am, a descendant of American Slaves, is more than mere fun —
it's a spiritual awakening, *it's uplifting*.

Tracing my roots *objectively* caused me to stop believing in the
fabricated lies our Uncle Tom leaders are continually passing on
to our people. I now believe in me — the real me. Believing in
myself made me to believe in my people. I am now firmly connected, and I will never let go. I am now drawing from my
ancestors the understanding and internal strength I had been
missing. My eyes are wide open, and my mind is receptive to all
things positive that will advance my people.

Since I found my true identity, I don't have that empty, nagging
inferior feeling anymore because now that I know who I am, I
also know why the feeling was there in the first place. And it
makes me feel so much better knowing the defect wasn't in me
or my kind. All of my life I have felt lesser because people of my
racial group are treated that way. My new awakening made me
understand there has never been any reason for me, or any other
descendant of American Slaves, to go my whole existence feeling
inferior to other human beings, especially whites.

It's a terrible thing knowing that something is wrong and not
know the truth of what it is. I had been thinking the fault was
in me because I was propagandized into believing the game was
fair — every man according to his abilities. For some reason, I
thought because I was 'colored,' which is what we descendants
of slaves were once called, my life was supposed to be more difficult than that of whites. At that time I had no idea why I
thought that way, but after I came to realize my identity, I knew
why. This assumption is an inherited carryover from slavery —
it's an aftereffect! That's the way slaves felt during slavery. Slaves
felt they were lesser than whites because that's the way whites
programmed their slaves to feel. That's the way whites treated
all slaves and *that treatment still exists today*.

All of my life I accepted this slavery mind-set without question. This stopped me from thinking about why the deck is

stacked against people who look like me in the first place.

Once I learned how to think instead of accepting things as they are I started looking for reasons, postulating that maybe I was being punished for something my ancestors had done wrong when they were slaves. But, I remember what my parents taught me: Never blame others for your failings. This started me thinking: Could the failure be in me, personally? Could I be overly sensitive? I searched within myself, but found no fault related to me being overly sensitive about my people's problem in America. If anything I was under-sensitive according to the injustices being dumped on my people. Even though the answers were slow in coming, I was determined to keep searching.

There's a pony in here somewhere

When the average slave who escapes the ghetto comes back to the 'hood, they are usually just visiting, not looking for answers. They wouldn't recognize the aftereffects of slavery because it can't be seen at a glance. The average runaway doesn't really know what to look for anyway. Most of the time fame and fortune have blinded our role models. When they visit the 'hood, they take what they *think* is a good look at ghetto misery. However, instead of seeing misery they, like as not, label the oppressed and overwhelmed as "trifling niggers." They are glad they got out and wonder why the slaves who got left behind don't do what they did — get the hell out! Does it cross the minds of the lucky few, the famed and fortunate that, except by the Grace of God, they could be right where most still are. These powerful slaves must understand that we can't get out. Ignorance has us locked in. Bigotry has blocked every exit and, besides that, where would we go and how would we get there? We don't have an escape route or a destination!

I took a closer look and it startled me. Everyone, including me, had abandoned these people. I really didn't know them anymore, and this included some of my own kin. At first, I actually regarded these abandoned people the same way I heard bigots express their feelings toward "lazy, no-good niggers." Once I got a good look and realized what I was looking at, it hurt me to think that perpetual discrimination had caused most of the people I left behind to give up all expectation of having a chance to win in life, or share in the American dream. I hadn't even been outside of the neighborhood that long!

This let me know that my getting away from ghetto misery is what allowed me to be able to see ghetto misery clearly. Slipping through a hole in the fence and getting a chance to see up close and then experience how white people live, think, and organize their lives, gave me the opportunity to compare my ghetto life, as a descendant of American Slaves, to that of free whites and how they conduct themselves.

Our two cultures suffer from ignorance, but in different ways.

Once I had escaped the 'hood, it took an ample amount of time for me to see and understand how corporate America works. Using hindsight, I realize it took just as long for me to really see and understand the suburbs clearly. However, after being gone from the 'hood for a while, it took even more time for me to get a real good look at my own old neighborhood again.

The difficulty in seeing whites clearly is because they have always tried to cover up their shame of slavery. Because of this shame, it's difficult to see slaves clearly. We are busy covering up the shame and misery that slavery left behind. It takes an ample amount of time to see what was intentionally hidden by whites then and is being unconsciously hidden by descendants of slaves today.

Well-to-do descendants of slaves think we are "seeing" our old 'hoods when we come back for a visit. This is hardly true. To see ghetto misery after you have been gone awhile and have risen in the ranks, you have to go back to the 'hood and live there.

When I was living there initially, everything seemed normal to me. I was just another young Negro boy who went happily about my life, and other colored people went about theirs. We instinctively did whatever we had to do to survive, one day at a time, because that's the way it was *and still is.* We never debated why people who looked like us were constantly abused; we just knew we were, and still are. Being abused is an established way of life for

> *"We never debated why people who looked like us were constantly abused; we just knew we were, and still are. Being abused is an established way of life for slaves. There has never been anything we could do about our maltreatment, so we have adapted. I now understand — that is what mental enslavement in America is all about."*

slaves. There has never been anything we could do about our maltreatment, so we have adapted. I now understand — that is what mental enslavement in America is all about.

Descendants of slaves don't reason why we expect other nationalities to be in charge of our lives — we just know they are. Few slaves know we are supposed to be in charge of our own lives in order to seek out our fair share of America. We don't understand that we could, and should, compete for American wealth as a group.

By re-acquainting myself with my people, I discovered few slaves even try to win at the game of life. There are some who have escaped from the 'hood and are hailed as being successful but, on moving up the ladder, they no longer feel a responsibility toward the rest of us even though we might have helped them along their way. The average slave is left to struggle alone and try to make ends meet, hope to survive, and someday be free of white oppression.

After talking to a number of slaves, I arrived at a surprising conclusion — they would just like to be able to enjoy some of life. Mostly, they want white folk to leave them alone for a while so they can find a little peace and happiness in this world. After digesting that bit of information, I understood that's the way *my* folks felt. That's why we left Georgia, in fear, *in the middle of the night.* That's really the way I felt when I was living in Eddy Alley but, because society programmed me to think that living in trepidation is 'my place,' *I thought I was having fun!* Consequently, before I moved to the suburbs, I never had anything to compare fun or freedom to. Now I know why I was a hell-raiser. I was a slave, living in mental hell, but I didn't realize it until I got a 'bankroll' fat enough to allow me to move to 'white folks' heaven.' A change of scenery to a place without ghetto influence allowed me to make a true comparison.

We have all heard the cliché, "Idle hands are the devil's workshop." Well, without adequate leadership and not enough decent jobs available to our kind, the average slave is idle; he does whatever comes up. Living in the 'hood, most of the time the wrong thing usually comes up and, being slaves, we are adaptable. We quickly adjust to the wrong situation.

Stifled dialogue

*A*merican Slaves never talk intelligently to our role models about racial abuse. Rather, we prefer to hide the abuse that is being dumped on us, sometimes even from our own. We are ashamed for our role models to know our true condition, because the majority of us think our dire situation is entirely our own fault.

We have a serious problem here because the average descendant of slaves who considers himself a 'role model' doesn't really want to come back to the 'hood anyway. If we start whining and complaining to them about how grim our situation is, or burdening them with problems about our racial condition, it's a good bet they will not return anytime soon and only then for a much shorter visit. Ordinary slaves must understand this 'role model' *doesn't know how to help us*; he just recently escaped poverty, himself. He probably won't be back anytime soon because *no one* appreciates being handed a problem that they have no idea how to solve.

At first, I didn't want to believe what was coming into view. Some of these people used to be my "running buddies." I came back to my 'hood for one single reason, and that was to take a *racial* look. I needed 'grass roots' reality. I wanted to compare those I had left behind to my newfound white friends; I needed to know why immigrants and foreigners are treated better than me and my people in our homeland. The only way I could get an answer to my uncertainty was to compare my part of the human race to that of other racial groups now residing in America.

Well, I did, and I saw a discrepancy. Something was missing among my people. At first, I couldn't put my finger on it. Then it hit me: *Overall — my people don't harbor hope.*

Slaves usually behave the way we think people from other groups expect us to conduct ourselves. We try to put on our best face, but it's hard to keep a game face continually because, every now and then the wear and tear on the heart causes a frown to appear on the face.

Studying it over, I saw that whites have hope — they exude hope. Comparing 'white hope' to slave descendants' lack of it, the picture became clear: Whites have avenues available to them where they can put their hope to work. The majority of descendants of slaves don't have hope, and even those of us with higher expectations lack avenues through which we can put that hope to work. Without advancement avenues hope usually turns into frustration and frustration to unrest. ❖

CHAPTER 19

It's Just Business

(The "good ol' boy" syndrome
in America is no myth)

I t's unfortunate that African American leaders have never understood the word 'hope' and what it means in the business arena in conjunction to descendants of slaves. Hope is what freedom is built on. Business is the lifeblood of freedom. The thirst for freedom is the driving force behind business. If business is carried out properly, it becomes a perpetual power; freedom becomes a byproduct of this exertion.

"Once we have an authentic leader, he should direct those under him to work toward strengthening those slaves who are in a position to become captains of industry, so they can, in turn, employ our people"

Hope is a powerful, motivational force, and it's missing among my people. Successful descendants of slaves must be mentally transformed first. They must be regenerated and made to see the big picture. Hope springs from above.

Once we have an authentic leader, he should direct those under him to work toward strengthening those slaves who are in a position to become captains of industry, so they can, in turn, employ our people — not so they themselves can become individual profiteers. Presently, our leaders 'think too small.'

The reason individuals in our group get misused when we do get a chance to participate in the American dream is because, even if we did have a winning plan, we don't belong to a definable racial entity that can back our hand. Without racial support, we become desperate to advance our personal plans and ideas. We lose hope, and ensuing panic makes us easy prey.

Descendants of slaves are sometimes forced into situations that allow whites and foreigners to increase their wealth at the expense of our people. The white race can still purchase us, and our ideas, for a fraction of what we are worth, just like they did during slavery.

On the other hand, whites can't be purchased as cheaply because they understand 'strength in numbers.' They draw strength from helping their own kind. They love doing favors, *so they can call in their markers.* This is how the "good ol' boy" routine works.

I'm just telling it like it is

It's hard to accept descendants of slaves who make it out of the ghetto enjoying their measly, material trappings knowing the condition they left their loved ones in. How can those who believe they are well thought of now, but lived in substandard conditions most of their lives, get a glimpse of what white freedom looks like, change their identity, and then suddenly discard any concern for helping those they left behind? I just don't believe America's Slaves would be that kind of people if they knew their history, accepted who their ancestors were, who they are, and what we as a people could become. Those of us who have made it out of the ghettos are the ones in the best position to change the ghettos. Who else to nourish hope?

Going the Distance

White leaders have the might, muscle, and intelligence to help us, but is it possible they might not know we want help? 'African American' leaders have positioned themselves between us common slaves and the white power structure. They are in a position to assist us, the same as white politicians help their people, but they refuse to even acknowledge us. That's why American Slaves are never heard from. That's also why we call our Uncle Tom politicians 'gate-keeper.'

Those who are left behind can wish for change, but they can't visualize how to get themselves from where they are to anywhere else. They are really unaware of what it takes to initiate so drastic a change.

A few who have 'made it' still live in the 'hood, and there are those like myself who have moved back into the inner-city. We are often times heard bragging about coming back to the 'hood to help our people, but if we studied ourselves and the situation before us, we would see that, we are not 'back' and we're not helping much of anyone, especially our people. When we rose, we

"How can those who believe they are well thought of now but lived in substandard conditions most of their lives, get a glimpse of what white freedom looks like, change their identity, and then suddenly discard any concern for helping those they left behind?"

not only separated ourselves from the lowest of our people physically, we left them behind *mentally*. To move up in life, it was necessary that our mentality be upgraded. That was the only way we could rise above poverty. We fail to understand that *ordinary slaves haven't been elevated*. And our not understanding this means our own progress is not yet complete. We can be back in the 'hood physically but our Uncle Tom mentality could still be intact. We can't help our people until we fully comprehend our people's true condition, comparatively. We will never understand our people's true condition, until we see that we are a real part of these people. We must put our arrogance aside and know that our good fortune was luck; that we are still slaves. Only after we understand who we are will we realize when we help our people we're really helping ourselves and the offspring of our nation.

Some wealthy slaves still remember what ghettos are like. We know it's 'a mind thing,' and we know what it took for us to get out. Those we left behind, some of whom live right around the corner from us that we see and speak to every day, don't know an escape route — *how could they?* These people haven't experienced the many ups and downs that some of us have; they haven't had a peek into the white, free world that some of us have observed. Simply put — *they don't know what we know.* If we were paying attention, those of us who have survived and sometimes thrived, should have learned many things that could help our people advance. It is what we learned on our way up that relieved us of ghetto misery and allowed us to advance. We can give back to our people by using what we have learned.

If I can change, other slaves can, too. I am now an American Slave who has not only gained valuable knowledge that could go a long way in freeing my people, I have acquired a "white business" mentality.

This realization not only gave me a mission, it gave purpose to my life. There are other descendants of slaves who have acquired white business mentalities. They could join me in this undertaking because this task should be their mission, also. It's time we came together and learned how to help our own; that's the only way we will ever be able to 'give back' to our people. It is also time for one of us to take over where Dr. King left off, but this time we must use the democratic process to elect that person.

> *"It's time we came together and learned how to help our own; that's the only way we will ever be able to 'give back' to our people. It is also time for one of us to take over where Dr. King left off, but this time we must use the democratic process to elect that person."*

Dr. King gave all he had for his people. He gave his life for us when we thought we were Negroes. Before he departed this life, he made it clear that if we wanted to be truly free, our next battle would be fought on the economic battlefield.

The economic arena taught me that the American dream is about people amassing wealth. Combining these two facets it follows that, for slaves to gather racial wealth, we *must* have a plan for that purpose. Now, keep in mind, we are living in a brand new era. Emotional demonstrations might have got us thus far, but this is a *whole new day*. When we step onto the economic battlefield, rational thinking must become our weapon of choice. ❖

America's Little Black Book

CHAPTER 20

Reparations War
(Eliminating the threat)

Perhaps, needless to say, doubletalk has already entered the reparations picture. Descendants of slaves are already being squeezed out of being recognized because we are not accurately identified, which means the slave nation won't be compensated.

Instead of it being restitution *to* descendants of American Slaves for their foreparents being enslaved, it is now simply "reparations for slavery." If we are not properly recognized and strongly organized, who knows what segments of the population might collect reparations for slavery.

Looking ahead

Trying to recompense the descendants of slaves through our government would be next to impossible, if not downright disastrous. Think about it. Who would get what? Would a slave descendant's mother get a bigger share than him? What if only his mother's side of the family descended from slaves and his dad was, say, a Cherokee Indian? What if his grandmother came here from Ireland well after the cover up of slavery was started? Would certain whites merely be partially liable? Would certain slaves get just partial reparations?

Who would actually get a slice of the reparation pie? How big a slice? Who gets no pie? Who pays the bill? Who doesn't have to pay for the pie? Who neither pays nor gets any pie? Do Native

Americans help pay for the pie — or get themselves a slice? How about mixed races and multinationals? And, how in the world would we decide just how big this pie will be? What is the dollar amount to adequately cover reparations? There are a great many mixed nationalities residing in America. Not all nations whose people have immigrated here had anything to do with slavery.

In a court of law, our current leaders' whole argument for reparations would fall like a house of cards in a windstorm when we get down to specifics. What if the direct descendants of a wealthy plantation owner lost the family farm in bankruptcy? Are they off the hook? Who gets to be God and make these decisions about whose pockets reparations come out of and whose pockets it goes into?

At first glance, the average person would conclude that the logistics of slavery reparations seems impossible, but there are sensible answers to restitution for slavery that can be easily applied. For starters, reparations are due only to the descendants of American Slaves — others need not apply.

I don't have a pat answer on how to help all descendants of slaves in all areas because, as of yet, all of the questions haven't been asked. However, because of my experience in business I do have a plausible solution to direct American Slaves headlong into the American mainstream. We descendants of slaves must help ourselves. We must stand up proudly and be who we are, and then we must collectively chart our way out of our predicament.

I know many slave descendants are not going to like these next words, but we must be clear on this. Our racial reparations are not to be wasted on piecemeal programs, nor is our compensation to be enjoyed by us, at present. It is to be used by our leaders to ensure that our entire ethnic population will have opportunities in the future, which brings us to another problem — trust. Slaves are apprehensive about trusting another slave with their money, or the future of our people, and I understand why. All you have to do is look at our current leaders.

It's vitally necessary that slaves be able to choose their own leader. We need to keep in mind, however it is still up to us to hold all of our leaders accountable. No matter who our leaders are, we must make sure they do their jobs properly and protect our American Slaves' birthright.

Descendants of slaves need a trustworthy, elected leader our people can control or else freedom will remain just out of our reach.

We 'cut our teeth' during our integration battle. It is now time to sacrifice again in preparation for the future. Our leaders must not do what some whites predict they will do, which is act like greedy, naive children and squander our inheritance, with the less fortunate of us meeting back at the welfare office wondering what happened.

Slave leaders must learn to think along these lines. They must be able to draw up a plan that will show clearly the steps to be taken for our people to achieve true freedom and how they are going to guide us through these steps. They must be able to properly explain to all American Slaves that our problems may not be cured in our lifetime.

We, descendants of slaves, must be made to understand that our immediate sacrifice of any such *individual* reparations (which is another way of saying welfare) could save and then secure our slave nation for all time.

When (*as a collective force*) we step into the economic arena, descendants of slaves must fully understand that white America caused our destitution because whites have always controlled the U.S. economy. However, when we get ready to do battle in the economic arena — *they are not the enemy*. American Slaves will need whites' loyalty, support, friendship, and help. The enemy is those who would oppose true freedom for our 'nation,' *no matter their color*.

We must think about ourselves as a collective, ethnic entity if we are ever to be an effective force, or a recognized part of America. Let us embrace our true selves, our genuine heritage. We are American Slaves!

Wasting restitution for slavery

*T*hose whites who do care, and those few slaves who have gained some intelligence, influence, and wealth, must participate in the true liberation of American Slaves. It's necessary to understand that American Slaves' planning for a bright future does not mean today's descendants of slaves will reap the reward, personally, and it does not mean that we as individuals will live to see the recompense gathered in. What it does mean is if we plan our work, do our part, and then leave our progeny a well-written constitutional document they can follow, every offspring of all American Slaves will at least have the opportunity to share in our birthright. Only through our inheritance, and only if it is handled properly, will every descendant of American Slaves (not just the offspring of our modern day Uncle Toms) have an opportunity to inherit the American dream.

If we ever expect to get serious about the welfare of our people, all American Slaves must go in the same direction. It's the only way we can have a true leader and, I reiterate, there can only be *one* commander in chief.

Competing harmoniously

*D*escendants of slaves love to compete, but because we are ashamed of who we are, we would rather compete on an individual basis — not as a racial group — because it's our group we are ashamed of.

Presently, and because we don't know any better, our competitive spirit leads slaves to subconsciously hope other individuals in our own racial group *lose*. If others in our racial group win, our ignorance makes us think we lose. The reason slaves hope other slaves lose is because we know once a slave becomes a successful African American he will forget about the common people and look down his nose at us as if we are 'beneath him.'

African American leaders don't really understand the full significance of team and teamwork. This causes descendants of slaves to not realize they are a part of a team of slaves. We have never functioned as a team; so ordinary slaves don't even try to pull together as a team. It's inherent that we pull *against* each other because of the divisiveness that was instilled into our being. This divisiveness perpetuates our struggling alone.

The problem with slaves learning to pull together is that we, as slaves, don't have an avenue by which we can acquire a leader of our choice. Not having a chosen leader, and with no personal agenda, we don't have anyone to tell us truthfully what is available to us.

The impossible made easy

Knowing the estranged condition of American Slaves, it would seem impossible to create a suitable communication channel to serve our needs. However, there is a spark of hope. Despite our racial division, we still come together at different times in small groups.

To start a communication channel that all slaves can utilize, the heads of each group of slaves (and this includes our churches) should decide what their group agendas are. Then they should get together and decide what the slaves' overall needs are in relation to the group agendas. Next, find a common denominator which should be a direction beneficial to all slaves and all groups and before proceeding further, *elect ourselves a leader*. It's the only way we can start ushering every slave, clique, group, and person collectively in *one* direction.

It's a must that we involve the leaders of the many small groups of African Americans, Negroes, blacks, and coloreds who might operate independently in the early formation and planning for our future. This would ensure that our one leader is chosen by the people, by popular vote.

To be successful in the industrial arena, we must address an important task that has been missing from our slave community since our inception — developing the American Slaves business community and helping slaves who are businesspersons strategize and draw from each other. ❖

CHAPTER 21

Minority Programs

(State-of-the-art doubletalk)

American Slaves have always been severely handicapped. Common sense tells us that, while other ethnic groups exist and have their own agendas, American Slaves are the only group in America that needs and deserves help from our government — as payback for the forced labor of slaves during slavery. This alone should justify the descendants of slaves having an exclusive help program.

"America's primary obligation should be to her only offspring, American Slaves. Omitting slaves, or mixing us in with all the other nationalities that are rushing into our homeland, without acknowledging who we actually are, keeps us almost invisible."

Our leaders' denying their identity causes our group to remain unrecognized. Any financial help that would be forthcoming to our people by way of government grants, business 'set-asides,' or government-sanctioned funds that could be tied to reparations for slavery, is diverted to minorities, foreigners and Uncle Toms. This miscarriage of justice forces a large number of our people to rely solely on the white race for welfare.

Did you know?

Even though slaves have always been on the bottom of American life, average slaves still think they are better than whites. This is an unconscious carryover from slavery. When slaves think we are better, we are thinking *individually* and *morally*. Our underlying slave mentality knows that whites are the perpetrators of slavery. We know we haven't done anything *morally* wrong.

American slaves must be made aware that we are not better than whites. In the industrial arena, the movers and shakers consider descendants of slaves the worst of the lot because we are not properly represented. We are thrown in with the leftovers at the bottom of the 'minority barrel.'

Minority programs do serve a definite, legitimate purpose; however, when it comes to the descendants of slaves, they are largely ineffective and subject to corruption. The problem is that most every individual in America, other than white American males, wishing to advance in American life financially or share in the American dream commercially, can be certified as a minority. This allows one to receive financial help, guidance, and business direction from our government through minority programs.

Because of discrimination and corruption, minority programs do little to help the descendants of slaves. These business programs have so diluted their impact as to be almost useless to us.

America's primary obligation should be to her only offspring, American Slaves. Omitting slaves, or mixing us in with all the other nationalities that are rushing into our homeland without acknowledging who we actually are, keeps us almost invisible. There is no program specifically designed for or dedicated to, the continued emancipation and upgrading of the descendants of American Slaves. Pretending to assist the descendants of slaves with generic set-aside clauses in a minority program is misleading and should be considered criminal.

Any plan backed by a program intended to help slaves, or their descendants, should say, "Descendants of American Slaves, *only.*" American Slaves deserve a bona fide help program that deals *exclusively with our special needs.* No other ethnic group should benefit from, or be included in American Slaves' tightly supervised ethnic program. This program cannot be another minority program — it must be an *American Slaves* program.

Program Incentives

*B*efore many immigrants get to America, they have seen on TV the way America treats American Slaves. This causes many of these immigrants to have a negative attitude toward the descendants of slaves before they even enter this country.

Should we expect otherwise? After all, in a sense they are the cream of the crop. First off, immigration in itself is a very influential screening factor in that only the most ambitious and assertive of foreigners are able to immigrate into America, legally. That is, the sluggards and ne'er-do-wells are still back in their native countries, sometimes living in mud huts and perhaps daydreaming of migrating no farther than to the nearest city in their own land. Thus, only a choice group of foreigners have the wherewithal and the resources to leave their native countries. It stands to reason that these ambitious and motivated, select few would hardly have made the trip here to just lie down and do nothing; they could have done that in their own country.

Thus, descendants of slaves are not competing against just average members of other nationalities, but rather some of the best educated, wealthiest, and most determined of those population groups. I expound on this so the reader will appreciate that American Slaves are not competing with just anyone. We are not only contending with highly inspired white Americans, we are competing against the very best people that other countries have while we are submerged in 'estranged ignorance' and without adequate leadership.

Once we have legally and successfully formed ourselves into a cohesive body, fair-minded politicians and aggressive leaders should assist us in coming up with a bona fide program for descendants of slaves. They should insist that tax incentives be given to corporations that adopt, financially support, merge with, or help develop slave-owned companies, thereby helping our sector of the human race grow.

Special tax incentives could be given to slaves' companies that merge with each other. The whole world is merging, but we're still adhering to the masters' rules that were handed down to us from slavery. During slavery, the master didn't want our foreparents to share information with each other; therefore, it was illegal for slaves to ban together and, until this day, *we still stay divided.* Slaves are not taking advantage of one of our greatest freedoms: *our right to assemble,* so we can share information and ideas.

My first idea would be to create an *untainted* think-tank before we get too far down the road. We need to put into place the brainpower needed to get us up and going. We also need an adequate communication channel, a way to assure the masses of descendants of slaves that all of our leaders are all on the same page. I have no doubt that we can reach our destination if we have strong leadership, true direction, and the proper mode of transportation.

An adoption program

Once we are a recognized population, major corporations could be enticed to adopt companies that are owned by descendants of slaves. If major corporations could also be allowed to have a vested interest in these companies, our success in the business arena would be almost assured.

Slave companies that are adopted by major corporations could be obligated to hire and train other slaves. Together, they could participate in the systematic retaking of inner-city neighborhoods by initiating well-thought-out business opportunities and challenging programs run by slave leaders with business mentalities.

If for some reason whites should think that properly freeing American Slaves will cost too much, our plan must show clearly that our true freedom won't cost America; America would be paying a debt that is owed. Getting out of debt is the 'summit' of the American dream, plus slaves becoming a prosperous people would add more wealth to the American 'bottom line.'

To get us started on our way, our leaders must get creative about the future of our people. So far, slave leaders have shied away from trying new ideas that might advance our people. Business taught me that when old ways haven't yielded favorable results, we must try something different. This is America; wealth is everywhere, but our leaders are not creative at all about the advancement of our slave nation. They should realize that it's their job as leaders to invest in the future of our people first. The first investment in any venture is in thoughtful planning.

In order for our plan to work, we must utilize our hindsight to recognize the cause of our current stagnation. Then we must look ahead and understand the many obstructions that could cause our plan to bog down or fail. We must remove those obstacles.

Our entire population group is stagnant because those of us who are businesspersons aren't more assertive. We aren't bolder because we have no avenues available to us through which we can advance. Most of the time, we have our hand out begging white lending institutions for working capital.

The average descendant of slaves who is in business is lost, scared, confused, or depressed. I know, at times I've suffered from all of these conditions during my adult life and business career. It doesn't matter how much money slave businesspersons think they have, their handicap is that they can see no future because they don't fully understand their past.

Even though this knowledge is very basic, it is still relatively new to our way of thinking. And, because of shame and stubborn ignorance, the average slave who is in business, or in a leadership position, might reject this perspective. To their way of thinking, they already know who they are — they're African Americans — and they are already doing well by clinging to their African roots and endeavoring to sever all memory of their American roots. They may choose to keep their heads buried in the sand, or either look the other way and let the rest of us stay buried in perpetual ignorance. Ordinary slaves must be made aware that, if our leaders are too ashamed of us to recognize us and identify with us and too proud of themselves to ask for help for our people, our group will never get the assistance due to American Slaves. Ingrained shame and false pride by 'African American' leaders encourages slave descendants' racial ignorance to remain intact and our racial destitution to grow.

Well, who's really to blame?

It took a while, but I finally learned. Those descendants of slaves who are preachers, teachers, politicians, and businesspersons are also our racial leaders. They are at the forefront of our group; they get the recognition; they get the bulk of the money and, whether they know it or not, they have the connections. This makes them responsible for the welfare of their people. What happens to an ethnic group is a direct result of what their teachers teach, their preachers preach, who their politicians are, what legislation they introduce and, ultimately, what happens to businesspersons at the top of that group of people.

Now that I look back, I understand that most of the errors I made in business and in my personal life were because I didn't know who I was. Not knowing my identity, and not belonging to a bona fide ethnic entity, I couldn't live up to my God-given potential. If I had known this earlier in life, I would have begun sooner to do what our ancestors left for us to do.

If I had fully understood who I was when I first started in business, I would have played my hand a lot differently because I would have known what I had to work with. I wouldn't have spent the better part of my business life banging my head against a brick wall, simply because my ignorance wouldn't allow me to see the bricks.

> *"Ingrained shame and false pride by 'African American' leaders encourages slave descendants' racial ignorance to stay intact and our racial destitution to grow"*

In business, I was recognized as a minority, but I was taught to think and act as if I were a white man because it was white people who taught me to play my hand as a minority. I'm not white, but I am a lot more than just 'a minority.' Most everyone that I was working with understood who they were except me! I accepted the minority role because I had never seriously thought about my own identity.

Perpetuating ignorance

As it stands, most descendants of slaves who go into business are destined to fail because of plain naiveté. Those slaves who are successful in business or the political arena must be willing to contribute to the cause by sharing the secrets of their success with others of our racial group.

In the business arena, I saw right away that 'white luck' is nothing more than being properly prepared and willing to go the distance when opportunity raises its lovely head. However, life has always been more difficult for slaves because as a group, we have been denied adequate preparation. Therefore, 'slave-luck' in business is slaves sharing information, helping each other, persuading each other to try harder, and not being afraid of success, *or failure.* And, if we are willing to go the distance when opportunity arises, there is a good chance that slave businesspersons could also experience what we thought was unattainable — 'white luck.'

People from my old neighborhood know from whence I came and the bumpy road that I traveled, but others who know me from the business arena probably assumed I was thoroughly prepared for my business career. I was not.

The secret to my success in business lies in my getting fed up with being mistreated because I am descended from slaves. From that moment of realization it has been concentration, determination, and a measure of luck. Concentration did help me to see my situation, and determination is what helped me claw my way out of my lesser condition, so perhaps I manufactured a bit of that luck.

Reinventing the wheel

Let us take a closer look at this thing called luck to demonstrate that good luck is a byproduct of hard work, determination, and concentration. We will use my manufacturing career to demonstrate the power of luck and how it worked for me, an ordinary slave.

Whites heard that I was a hard worker, which is true. I get joy out of outperforming others, and I love doing a good job. These whites sought me out to be their minority manufacturer because this venture called for an up-and-coming slave who has an 'old-school mentality.' *In other words, a hard working 'minority' who is racially ignorant, but still, highly trainable,* a perfect Uncle Tom candidate.

After 'scoping me out,' whites wined me and dined me at the one of the finest restaurants. I was impressed and 'chomping at the bit.' I was ready even if I didn't get to break out of the gate just then. As the first meeting was winding down, they asked me if I wanted in and if I had any questions. I said, "I definitely want in and, yes, I do have a question: What does 'manufacturing' mean?"

I had seen the letters, "Mfg. Co." on buildings, but I had no idea what this signified. This will give you an idea how ignorant I was concerning manufacturing.

Even though I had already started several small, neighborhood businesses from scratch, when it came to America and American commerce at this height I was ignorant — I was easy prey.

Before whites thrust me into the manufacturing arena, we formed a legal corporation, me as president, not because I am descended from slaves (that was never mentioned) and definitely not because I was qualified because they knew I wasn't. Whites sought me out because I was the only one in this group who could be certified as a minority and because they had heard about my "never give up" attitude.

Like other descendants of slaves who out of the deep blue sky are offered the chance of a lifetime, I didn't even have the intelligence or take the time to ask these whites what being a minority meant; I was just pleased, proud, *and in a hurry* to be one. Amazingly, I was the answer to their needs. The person who thought up the idea became vice president, but this was a side agreement. I had no idea what I was doing or what he was doing. At this level in the business arena, they knew full well that I was "business illiterate."

Under watchful eyes, they carefully prepared me according to our new company's profitability expectations. Day and night they rehearsed and critiqued me to the point of exhaustion.

During corporal slavery, our foreparents were intensely prepared for servitude, and then they were introduced to America as slaves. Now I was being intensely prepared and introduced, but in a different way. When these whites felt I was ready, they introduced me to corporate America as a promising minority manufacturer.

I hit the floor running and put on the minority businessman performance of a lifetime, but I didn't have a clue how the outcome of the minority business deals I was involved with were impacting my segment of the human race. Looking back, I can see that ignorance had me running a 'front company' for whites, *and I didn't even know it.* I thought they were helping *me* because I was a minority. At that time, I didn't comprehend that the idea of minority programs was conceived as a means to repatriate descendants of slaves for slavery. These whites weren't helping me; they were helping themselves to American Slave's portion of the American dream.

Whites wanted to use me to make them more wealth, so they put me through a private, individual, business curriculum — the kind they don't offer in business school. It was to their benefit, financially, that these whites let me see and hear things that the average descendants of slaves couldn't have seen or heard. I imagine my situation was similar to Uncle Tom's situation during slavery times. During slavery, the master talked freely in front of a few selected slaves. Now, like some other slaves in business, I was in an Uncle Tom position, but I didn't realize it.

I admit freely that I have an inherited slave mentality, but fortunately I don't have an ingrained Uncle Tom attitude. I suppose most all of my ancestors were lowly field hands instead of 'house niggers.'

In business, timing is crucial. These whites were after a certain niche that was available in corporate America. A major manufacturer needed parts built by a minority manufacturer in order to get the best tax break. This contract, like all other contracts that are allotted to minorities, didn't mention descendants of slaves because we are not a recognized people nor are we a legalized entity.

When slaves were dumped out on their own after slavery, the

government made our foreparents start paying taxes, but that same government has never declared slaves human. This grievous oversight still hinders slaves, as a people, from being figured into the American tax structure. Therefore, we still don't get the racial consideration that recognized ethnic entities do.

Unaware 'wunderkind'

*U*sing intense grilling (and in record time), whites transformed my overall persona. They taught me how to dress, how to talk and walk but, most important, they taught me to think differently. I learned a lot from these whites. Among other things, I learned that we American Slaves are *a highly trainable people.* These whites said as much, but not in those exact words.

I must admit that, once entrenched, I did learn at an accelerated pace. It didn't take long at all for me to see what was going on around me. Not only did I stumble upon my identity, I came to understand how whites programmed our ancestors to be their slaves. In this venture, the lash and shackles weren't used, still these whites were programming me to be their slave. This would have been the perfect situation for them, *and me* if I had an ingrained Uncle Tom mentality.

It took some doing, and I went through a great deal of abuse, but I finally made it in the world of business. Once I began to understand how white folks think, my success was not only easy, it was, and still is, fun. I'm eager to share what I've learned, even while I'm still learning.

Whites purposely schooled me on what to watch out for in business and then they exposed me to the world of commerce. Once I had the game figured out, I compared black leadership to white leadership. When I saw how white leaders work together to get things done *for* their people, and how our leaders battle against each other because of ignorance, I realized the shabby job our leaders have been doing.

Not many of our 'African American' leaders have been taught by whites what I was taught, or the way I was taught it. Few of our leaders have been where I have been and seen what I have witnessed. If all descendants of American Slaves were allowed access to the information I was privileged to receive, our people would break loose and free — I sincerely believe this.

Now, let us use what hindsight we have gained. Before I knew who I was, I allowed devious whites to talk me into claiming that I was a minority — and I was proud to be one because, before I became a certified minority, I was thought of as nobody. I didn't even know there was such a thing as an "American economic mainstream." Now, all of a sudden, my first name is 'mister,' I'm on television giving interviews and even motivational talks to school children, as well as speaking to prisoners.

At that time, I didn't have proper knowledge to talk intelligently about the American dream. I was lecturing in ignorance. I didn't fully realize then what the American dream was all about, but now my eyes are opened. The American dream is big and it's available to all! The only thing holding American Slaves back is *inadequate leadership.* Imagine me, an 'alley rat,' a *dropout,* doing business with some of the biggest corporations in America and testing my newly acquired business skills against some of the most brilliant minds of the world and too ignorant to even know my true identity. That's how wide open the American dream is — I was hanging out with 'the big boys.'

Using me as an example, imagine what could happen if our leaders were to come together, figure out the 'game,' *outline our mission,* and then start working together as a team. Taking our knowledge and what our white brothers and sisters could teach us, we would show them that we are a deserving people; we couldn't help but have good luck.

It's true whites showed me how to get minority certification, then they taught me how to play the role. However they never told me that when a person is doing business and uses the word minority, it influences whatever business deal is being done. If claiming to be a minority, or having been certified as such, that person is not doing business for just himself, he is doing business for his people and in the name of his ethnic group. The word minority dictates how other ethnic groups deal with the person who is claiming that he is a minority; it impacts that person's group's well-being.

> *If claiming to be a minority, or having been certified as such, that person is not doing business for just himself, he is doing business for his people and in the name of his ethnic group.*

Who a person is when doing business in America is vitally important because all groups are perceived differently. They all have a different, unspoken level of status. *That's what discrimination is all about in America.*

My new status was 'minority manufacturer.' I somehow connected the word '*minority*' with who I am racially, but I was rudely awakened. I have always aspired to helping my people, but every time I wanted to use my newly acquired minority position in this manner, I was advised by my white mentors to keep a low profile and never to speak out on racial issues. They said it could hurt my chances at success and even destroy the company we had put together. That didn't sit well with me, but I had invested all of myself and every dime that I had into this company. The cards had been dealt and I had no choice but to play the hand out.

In the business arena, fear can be overwhelming. Fear of failure, fear of backlash from whites and slaves, and bad advice from over-protective mentors cause most descendants of slaves to be suppressed even on the executive level. Backlash would not only come from the people we are trying to help, but also from the white sector that we deal with and depend upon for our business survival.

When I was told by whites that it was best that I not get involved in racial matters, which meant I couldn't help my people, my attitude started a shift from positive to negative. In the everyday world, a negative mindset can be confusing to those around you. In the business arena, the distractions of this state of mind are compounded. A black person with a negative state of mind is a twofold annoyance to those in positions of authority. At first, it was merely my ignorance that was hurting my people. Now my ill-mannered attitude was turning whites off. Upon closer observation, I was not just some isolated, rebellious maverick. This problem is more serious than one might think. *American Slaves, as an entire people, inherited a depressed mindset*, causing our group to be caught up in a vicious circle of negativity.

It was in the manufacturing arena that I was forced to deal with my racially-inherited, negative state of mind. In coping with this, I not only broke free of the circle, I became a better businessperson. I also stumbled upon a deeper appreciation of my homeland, gained a clearer understanding of slavery, and I attained the peace of mind from which my ignorance had been robbing me.

All right, I've got my head on straight — what's next?

Because of my inherited mental programming, I was excessively grateful to these whites for giving me a chance to share in the American dream, even though I didn't understand some of the business deals they had me involved in. The whites who were using me didn't tell me everything. They told me only what they wanted me to know and hoped I'd never figure out the difference between the American public, the political community, and the American business arena, and how they connect.

Being in this upscale business environment, I was suffocating in my own ignorance. Grudgingly, I cast my fear and shame aside and trusted my instinct and kept trudging on. Fortunately, my determination to figure out the basics of American business triumphed over my inherited ignorance. I found out how and why business impacts differently on American population groups. I now believe in the American dream because I have seen it in action. I have lived it, but only a personal basis. Why shouldn't all of my people have at least a chance to live the American dream?

Other population groups take advantage of the opportunities that are available in America. They immigrate into America, ban together, and then prosper in our homeland. I firmly believe that if our leadership were to come together, and then learn how to work together for our common good, the entire American Slave nation couldn't help but benefit.

Before my indoctrination into the industrial world, I couldn't imagine why slavery had been so necessary to America, or how important my ancestors' roles as American Slaves were to the building of America. I had never visualized the entire business playing field from the commencement of the United States of America. I spent years parading as a minority, pleading for a chance to share in the American dream. Yet not once did I consider that my ancestors helped build the very country I was begging in. They weren't paid for their labor; that debt is still outstanding. It's owed to me and others like me who have spent the better part of our lives in dire poverty, we are the descendants of those slaves who helped build this nation.

It is because of the shame connected to slavery that I always shied away from thinking about my ancestors, or slavery, except in a casual way. I never realized the enormous profitability of slavery to the slave master then and, more important, how that same slavery is still crucial and can become profitable to the descendants of slaves today. My inherited ignorance wouldn't allow me to visualize my whole surroundings. This caused me to be subservient, docile, and then deferential, even when I wasn't supposed to be. Too often I gave in to unscrupulous whites and devious blacks when I should have held my ground.

Every descendant of American Slaves who is fortunate enough to be doing business in America, or has prospered in America, has a personal responsibility to our people. When descendants of slaves get lucky and prosper, but don't live up to their inherited responsibility, they are branded Uncle Toms, and rightfully so.

If our business and political leaders could approach this overlooked information with an open mind and then take the time to understand it, they would become aware of how they are hurting our community. If they would use this information properly, it could go a long way in liberating us from the prison of racial ignorance.

I went into business to better myself. I believed in the American system and our elected white leaders and self-appointed Negro leaders and what they told me, but to no avail. They actually had me believing that, if I worked hard, treated everyone right, obeyed the law, and did what they suggested, I would be treated equally because everyone is supposed to be treated fairly in America. Consequently, when I wasn't treated equally I would get frustrated and upset and this did damage to my self-esteem.

I looked around me and I wasn't alone. Others like me were being abused for the same reasons I was. This made me think something was wrong with all descendants of slaves because, as a group, we are treated differently from other racial groups — we are discriminated against. Discrimination caused me to become ashamed of myself and other 'colored people' who look like me.

Recognizing my true identity led to self-awareness. This new awareness helped me appreciate my meager trappings, compared to that of my immediate ancestors. I was able to compare the lack of advancement of my people, not only to the white race, but also to that of other population groups that have come into our country since slavery. It startled me. American Slaves have been in America longer than immigrants, yet immigrants have surpassed the descendants of slaves in most every aspect of American life. Many immigrants come right into our country, go straight to the front of the line leading toward the American dream, and, as often as not, start prospering immediately.

"American Slaves have been in America longer than immigrants, yet immigrants have surpassed the descendants of slaves in most every aspect of American life."

It hurt me deeply to realize that America, the country that slaves helped build (albeit a forced labor) would allow such an unfair practice, but then I realized immigrants don't really have to buck the freedom line, or squeeze in front of us to seek the American dream. The unfairness is not immigrants bucking the freedom line; the injustice is we aren't recognized. Therefore, we aren't considered — we aren't even in the line! It's white America's fault that American Slaves have never been recognized or treated fairly.

TV is constantly blaring that some immigrant groups now outnumber 'African Americans.' What bothers me is that American Slaves are standing by, watching our own demise, and we don't even realize what we are seeing.

The slave master knew then that our foreparents, freshly released from slavery and shackled with ignorance, weren't prepared to compete with them. White businessmen of today know that we are the descendants of those same slaves and, as a group, they know we still aren't able to compete. ❖

Chapter 22

Heaven on Earth

(Making preparation for the future)

To enter our people in the American dream line and make the legacy of slavery work to everyone's advantage, white and black, let's take a closer look with our clergymen first, because, when we get down to the real 'nitty-gritty,' they are our established leaders.

Churches are the most conspicuous symbols of hope in our race, and where we usually derive our leadership. However, our leaders must understand our people's needs. We need a single leader who is not afraid to aggressively address those needs. As of now there is no intermediary who negotiates, or speaks, for our people. None of our leaders, including the clergy, know they are supposed to be familiar with slavery or problems stemming from slavery. They don't know they are inherently responsible for what controls the racial destiny of American Slaves.

Laying the structural foundation

Slave leaders must start looking ahead. They must start thinking creatively about what steps to take to achieve *true* equality for the descendants of slaves.

Our most noticeable resource, even though divided, is our populace. Our spiritual leaders *direct the mentality* of our masses; however, for us to become a liberated people our politicians must learn to 'lobby' for our masses. To become a prosperous people, however, we would need our business leaders to employ the masses. This tells me that slaves need a workable conduit between politics, religion, and commerce. A political church business coalition must be formed to enable cooperation, but there must be a time limit to this alliance.

A time frame for the American Slaves' politics, church, and business to band together and, after a time, divide, is necessary, because of the condition of our people collectively. Slave churches are the wealthiest entity within our ethnic group, and slave politicians are connected to our white controlled system, but the overall state of our ethnic community is in financial quicksand. Therefore, it would be necessary and proper for our politicians to see that other slaves, besides just themselves, get connected politically. Churches, because of their monetary resources, need to get together with our business leaders and stand firm behind them, financially, until our business community is established and stable. Then, we would need to separate church and business, giving each sector the proper balance. In the long run, this would help strengthen our elected officials politically, our ministers' financial bases, and American Slaves' financial foundation. It would connect our community and give our business leaders the positive ingredient called racial backing.

Descendants of slaves who are our spiritual leaders are now building bigger churches. They are also soliciting more money from their flocks to pay for these edifices. This creates an additional drain on American Slaves' already weak economy because, even though our churches are wealthy, they don't utilize their wealth to employ but a handful of our people.

Let's do some business

Once slaves know who we are, and once we let America know that we recognize and accept who we are, the door to success will open wide for slave descendants. Toward that end, the United States owes descendants of slaves a running start — the generally accepted premise behind all minority pro-

"Slave churches are the wealthiest entity within our ethnic group, but the overall state of our ethnic community is one of financial quicksand. Churches need to get together with our business leaders and stand firm behind them."

grams. However, no matter where our restitution comes from, in the long run the astuteness of our business leaders will ultimately determine any rise in our standard of living. It's their job to look out for our financial well-being.

Churches would still be responsible for our spiritual well-being as our politicians would be for lobbying and then documenting our peoples' freedom properly. If the leadership of our group were to start working hand in hand, we would have three entities looking out for the overall well-being of our people with a clear mission and proper direction.

The ministers of our group must first learn the truth, and then they must preach the truth clearly. Our political leaders must start speaking up for us, and our business leaders must take it upon themselves to come together. The leadership of our slave nation must start showing some kind of spirit. They must start immediately training themselves mentally to know what to do with racial assistance once it is secured for us. Those who take credit for leading us must combine their minds and coordinate their efforts. Hopefully, the descendants of slaves who are clergy, politicians, and businessmen will understand the necessity of developing a *collective* 'business' mentality.

Unclogging the economic trickle-down

Usually, when American Slaves venture into business, their only promising source of receiving guidance, assistance, or support is from small neighborhood programs. However, such programs are not large enough to target a depressed section of the American population nationwide.

When our leaders allow the American system to waste funds targeting the masses of inner-city ghettos residents to receive racial help, they're wasting money because they are targeting the wrong end of our racial group. We live in a business environment, and whatever is happening in the ghetto is a result of what is happening at the top of the American Slaves' business world. The effect just manifests itself among the common of our people, or the weaker of our slave nation.

The trickle-down theory in economics is well established. In essence, it states that financial benefits accorded to the larger business enterprises will, in turn, pass down to smaller businesses and consumers, benefiting all people from the highest rung to the lowest. This is the justification offered for granting tax cuts to large businesses and keeping incentive programs alive that are supposed to help our inner cities, such as minority programs.

It stands to reason that if a ghetto business was owned by a descendant of slaves and helped to thrive through various incentives, considerations, and proper direction, it would not just pull up stakes and leave the blighted. A slave business would stay put, and even expand, if it were nurtured properly. Business expansions usually create new jobs and involve more people in a positive manner.

Now, let us look at the trickle-down theory in conjunction with dividing up reparations for slavery among the masses of descendants of slaves. If our reparations came to, say, 100 million dollars, and we were to give one million descendants of slaves 100 dollars each with which to do something good for their section of the American populace, could we expect anything noteworthy or memorable to come of it? Of course not. It would disappear overnight.

On the other hand, if we divided that same $100 million among 100 descendants of slaves who were allotted a million dollars each, and each recipient was directed how to spend it wisely for inner-city welfare and for the betterment of our people, just think of the good that could be accomplished with one million dollar infusions into 100 worthwhile causes or fledgling slave businesses that could be obligated to hire and properly train the unemployed, inner-city people.

Slave leaders' ignorance as to how commercial trickle-down works in America suggests that the only trickle-down American Slaves may ever receive is hand-me-down ignorance. City officials continually try to solve the slave descendants' problems without going to the source of the trouble. Slaves who reside in our inner-cities are routinely mistreated because seemingly *everyone thinks we're the problem!* Ghettos and slums that have an overabundance of rundown, abandoned buildings, with the majority of the residents collecting some type of subvention, are the result of our predicament, not the cause. Descendants of slaves are clearly the victims, not the culprits.

Mistreating our people won't improve our neighborhoods. And trying to help our masses, using insignificant neighborhood projects, when the leadership is so chaotic nationwide is putting forth a lot of local effort simply to prove that, when it comes to helping the descendants of slaves, futility exists in our country nationwide. ❖

CHAPTER 23

Divided We Fall, and Fall

(Investing in the future)

The slave nation must not waste any funds or effort on programs that have been tried before. Neither can we be hoodwinked into letting any forthcoming funds be divided up among the masses of us. This is extremely important! Emulating programs that have already failed is an ignorant act, and it guarantees the same failures. Dividing up our reparations among the masses of us would result in the funds dissipating within an embarrassingly short time span. Being a divided people and not a structured, productive nation, we are individual consumers, not organized producers. Therefore, the funds would be quickly consumed individually, but would not produce any meaningful or lasting results ethnically, racially, or commercially for descendants of slaves.

> *"Dividing up our reparations among the masses of us would result in the funds dissipating within an embarrassingly short time span."*

Another drawback to any funds being simply 'divvied up' among the masses of slave descendants is, of course, that most descendants of slaves couldn't produce legal proof connecting them to slavery if their lives depended on it.

Sure, we are descended

from American Slaves, but we can't document it. This is a part of our legacy. Although we don't have documentation proving we are slaves, if we recognize who we are and formally organize ourselves, the American Slave nation will have a better chance of getting collective justice — it's that simple!

Assertive leaders should welcome this form of sensible reparations for our people. However, due to shortsightedness, some African Americans may not see the logic in investing our reparations in the future of our nation or in slaves pulling together for our collective benefit. They must be told that upon the awakening of our people if it can't be explained properly how reparations for slavery will benefit our people now *and in the future*, mob violence could rule the day. Ordinary slaves will not understand (much the way they were bewildered when Dr. King was slain).

Upon Dr. King's death, our remaining leaders were in shock. None of them fully comprehended 'the American way,' nor the underlying hate derived from slavery. They didn't understand the widespread ignorance among our people. They didn't realize that ignorance is the spark that usually ignites smoldering hate into a flare-up of violence. They had no idea how to take appropriate measures to control the situation because they didn't fully understand why Dr. King was assassinated. Simply put, they weren't prepared. Hurt, confused, emotionally drained, and having no one we respected to tell us what to do, common descendants of slaves resorted to hostile behavior. The repercussions of mob violence never crossed our minds.

If we had known our collective identity, we would have understood that our leader was killed while trying to marshal his people into a unified force. It's clear to see that the assailants, whoever they were, were successful.

If the surviving leaders had been intelligent, and had devised a plan to follow, or even if they had been able to read between the lines of Dr. King's messages, racial rioting could have been avoided.

An authentic leader would have known how to use Dr. King's death as leverage, or as a stepping stone, to advance Dr. King's people closer to their goal. A perceptive leader would have known how to explain to his followers the harm that can come from a pointless riot. If we were bonded together and had proper leadership and a strong communication channel, across the board negotiations might have precluded the mob violence that followed our leader's death. We could have built on what Dr. King had accomplished and moved on down the road. Dr. King's death presented us with just the opportunity we needed, but our leaders couldn't think commercially.

If we have learned anything from the tragedy of 1968, it is the peril in not having proper leadership and a written plan to follow. There are explicit reasons why whites constructed the U.S. Constitution and have only one President who governs the other leaders. Yet, after all of this time, American Slaves still don't have a leader and no type of plan to follow. If reparations is ever to become a reality, proper leadership and an implementation plan is absolutely essential.

As an infant nation, we have managed to survive thus far. However, if we are to flourish, we must have a plan that will guide us through the uncertainties of maturing, and a leader who not only understands the plan but also appreciates racial evolution.

Money is not the answer

Our country's leaders must understand that someday the descendants of American Slaves will awaken and recognize themselves for what they are. When that happens, we must have a workable plan ready. We must be able to guide the descendants of slaves through uncertain times.

Philosopher/humorist Will Rogers is reported to have said, "Even if you are on the *right* track, if you just sit, a train will hit you." The time is now for American leaders to get together and develop a plan that we abandoned slaves can follow. Thinking creatively, America could gently awaken American Slaves by presenting them with this very special, timely gift of freedom. In due course, American Slaves would recognize the significance of such a development and be grateful. Our appreciation would strengthen America as well as enhance our country's racial image significantly.

To me, reparations for slavery is not about monetary restitution. Reparations for slavery should provide a well protected, adequately-funded, readily-available avenue that leads to all descendants of American Slaves being given a fair chance to share in the American dream. Once our leaders fully appreciate that we live in an industrial society, they will also understand that slaves learning how to work together as a team for their own good is not only proper reparations, it's the only way we can achieve true freedom.

Why should we wait for the government to help our people? We all know how slow our government can be, especially when it comes to helping slaves. There are enough rich descendants of slaves in America to start our own program, *with our own money* — that's what whites would do. That's what immigrating populations are doing as I put pen to paper.

Outlining recompense for American Slaves will require astute, fair minds that can think creatively and negotiate innovatively. Those few slaves who can think on their feet must cast aside their greed and fear; they must rise above being apathetic in regards to their people; they must come to the forefront of our slave nation to protect those of us who are not so blessed.

The invisible, internal war

I have talked to slave descendants about the possibility of their becoming front-runners in our reparations effort, but all have declined. Without openly saying it, they make it clear they have all but given up on their own kind. One slave descendant however, did speak bluntly: "Niggers will never, *ever* get together." This attitude is the reason why we don't even try to get together.

Those of us who have been beaten down by our own kind when we tried to help shouldn't despair nor should we give up. Getting knocked down doesn't mean we lost the fight — it means we're in a fight, and we may have to go the distance to win. Simply put, the majority of our people are lost in darkness. Those of us with a glimmer of understanding must try harder and think smarter. It's up to those of us who have seen the light to show the way to freedom.

> *Without openly saying it, they make it clear that they have all but given up on their own kind, but one slave descendant did speak bluntly: "Niggers will never, ever, get together."*

Some slaves, such as I, have lived on both sides of the fence. Some of us have experienced the underside of being poorly educated and disadvantaged. A few of us survived. We overcame that heritage in order to reap the benefits of success in the same white, dominated world that enslaved our people, but we didn't do it by ourselves. Whether we admit it or not, every slave who has 'made it' in America received some type of help from a white person.

Keep in mind, if our people are to advance into the American, socioeconomic mainstream of America, our white brothers and sisters must bless our entrance. ❖

CHAPTER 24

Getting to Know White Folk

(Understanding the white mindset)

Some whites will swear that they know our people and are sensitive to our needs. I know they mean well but, because they can never feel the pain of slavery, they can't understand our true mental condition, nor can they understand slaves' underlying disgust for whites even we don't fully understand. Therefore, they can't know our integral needs. Whites are not the survivors or victims of slavery; they are the beneficiaries of slavery.

In David Horowitz's book, "Uncivil Wars," he states that all people should be judged on their merit, not as members of a racial group. It appears this author has found a false comfort zone, and his position would be fine if all things were equal, and if American Slaves weren't so identifiable.

If American Slaves are forever thought of as individual African Americans and not as a racial group of slaves, our

"The idea that whites work together like ants or bees contributing to the common good to do what's best for whites, or that they follow some secret rules for the betterment of "whitedom" is a mistaken fantasy."

slave nation will never get the direct assistance that is due our people. This means that only the few of us who are singled out, accepted, and then liked by certain whites within the system, will have a chance at success. Mr. Horowitz seems to think that if individual slaves *are* judged by *their* merit, and then awarded according to *their* personal ability, the slave nation has been dealt justice. That's backward thinking, or it's another sarcastic way of overlooking or omitting the American Slaves as a distinct American population.

Mr. Horowitz also said that Illinois didn't have anything to do with slavery, so he doesn't understand why Chicago Mayor Richard Daley apologized for slavery.

According to what America stands for, and given that we are all human beings no matter our color, and realizing that we all must live here in America together, it makes perfect sense that white leaders with common decency should apologize for their people's wrongdoings. If the original American Slaves had manipulated innocent minds, tortured and killed childlike humans for profit, and were still enjoying the rewards of their race's evilness, apologizing would be the least any decent person would do, especially if he calls himself a leader.

When Mayor Daley apologized for the immorality committed by his racial group, it proved that he not only had hindsight but he was a clear thinking, farsighted leader because he was looking down the road.

There are many nationalities living in Chicago. Mayor Daley was leading all of them. Being an astute leader, he must have known some of these people were descendants of slaves. He understood that even a simple apology could help pave the way for a peaceful, future coexistence between people who have deep-rooted, racial differences.

Mayor Daley recognized wrong done by his own group and apologized for it to the many groups that were following him.

Mayor Daley showed that he had the backbone to stand firm for what is right, even in the face of adversity. What a contrast to the weak politicians who usually bend too easily under a small amount of pressure.

Untangling the white conspiracy myth

For the descendants of slaves to gain full participation in the American economic mainstream, it will be necessary for our leaders to understand the opposition they will encounter. To understand that which is misunderstood, the first thing we must do is cast some doubt on our own wisdom. The typical African American leaders think they understand white folks. Judging from their actions, and our current condition, I am here to tell them: No, you don't!

Really understanding whites will be one of our most enlightening awakenings. The first thing our leaders should learn to perceive is 'white doubletalk.' Then they must learn to think like whites, so they will at least understand how whites think, simply because whites hold the reins of power. Now, I know the masses of our people. Because of our inherited ill feeling toward whites, most will say, "I don't want to think like whites; they're mean and evil."

This is not universally true, of course. Yes, there are some evil, lowdown whites, but they are a minority. We must keep in mind: It is because of our inherited disgust towards those 'hooded midnight riders,' the 'Hitler Brotherhood,' and others that slaves have a tendency to think all whites are evil. Whites, by and large, are not evil. They may at times be fooled with doubletalk by a crooked politician and consequently elect an evil leader, and then have no choice but to follow that elected leader. That aside, it's more important that we are clear on this — average whites are business-minded and American Slaves are not. Commerce was not a part of our inherited mentality.

Commercial thinking, in regards to our people's well-being, is something that our leaders must become skilled at.

Sometimes what slaves consider 'white evilness' is whites demonstrating their inherited business mentality. It took a while, but I learned the hard way that a business mentality doesn't harbor personal feelings, or emotion, and won't tolerate disarray. Slavery was, and still is, hard-core, heartless business, and whether whites know it or not, that's the way they are looking at slavery when they claim they didn't have anything to do with it.

Because of their inherited mindset, some whites may not understand how to be compassionate toward slaves. One of our biggest challenges will be teaching white Americans how to show compassion to their darker skinned-kinfolk, whom their people have abused, but not by way of pity. *Slavery needs to be understood.*

To think like whites, our leaders must stop thinking emotionally and learn to think logically, commercially, and racially. Yes, whites do think racially, or along color lines. If they didn't there would be no need for me to write a book of this nature because whites wouldn't have made dark-skinned humans into slaves in America.

Thinking racially is not such a bad thing if the thoughts are timely and honorable. *Not* being able to think racially could be considered disastrous, especially if it's required in the midst of a racial dilemma and the problem solvers are not honorable and their timing is off. To me thinking racially is simply seeing different racial groups of people as they are or, in a simpler term, seeing human life as it is. Timing in a racially explosive matter is doing something about a bad situation while there is still time — before it gets out of hand.

When thinking *racially,* in regard to the descendants of American Slaves, the first thought that comes to my mind is that American Slaves are not a *recognized* part of the human race; therefore, we get no *racial* consideration. My second concern is to figure a way to form our slave nation, legally. It's the only way slaves can ever be accepted into the American scheme of things or get consideration. A third idea is to draft a concrete racial plan that defines short-term, intermediate and long-range goals that will advance our people once we are in the main-stream. In an industrial arena, these are the kinds of commonsense concerns that a leader of slaves needs to address.

> *"Sometimes what slaves consider 'white evilness' is whites demonstrating their inherited business mentality."*

How could a descendant of slaves think he is a politician and not lobby for an American Slave program for his people? It's shameful that none of our current leaders have thought of this *basic* maneuver.

Trying to influence legislators or other public officials in favor of upgrading their people's standard of living should be a no-brainer for descendants of slaves who think they're politicians and call themselves leaders.

Racial love

Our leaders being educated in American ways, and white mentalities is only two of three lesson they must learn before we can move forward. It is more important that they learn to love their ethnicity and then illustrate to the masses of American Slaves how to love each other, collectively. This will be an emotional, cultural 'high,' an entirely new experience. Most of us think we are experiencing ethnic love when we feel a disturbing, emotional sensation toward other dark-skinned individuals who are suffering the same abuse as we are, but that's merely sympathy. To love who we are *as a people*, we must first recognize *who we are* and then we must become familiar with our true roots, which are entrenched in slavery in America. Purely and simply, we must learn to love American Slaves.

Unfortunately, we are 'slave haters,' but once we fully understand the high price that our foreparents paid for us even to be here — *how can we not love them?* Once we understand the tough job that lies ahead for all slaves, we had better learn to love each other if we want to succeed.

The most difficult obstruction standing in the way of slaves learning to love who we are is that 'African American' leaders would have to do a complete racial turnaround and admit that they are American-bred — descendants of slaves. And that's asking a lot from leaders who are invested in ignorance and blinded by petty success. These leaders will probably argue that going back to slavery and starting all over again will put us further behind. I would remind them, we don't have to *go back* to slavery; our nation has always been mentally enslaved.

When a group of people are going in the wrong direction and then begin to realize it, turning back to get an accurate start is the only sensible route to advancement, and it's not that far back. It just involves some clear, positive thinking by those who would lead us.

Our leaders must stop making slavery a negative part of our being. They must 'flip the script' and make it a crucial, but positive, focal point of our future existence *because that's what it is!* We can't undo slavery, but we can get our heads together and learn how to make slavery work in our favor.

The time is right for American Slaves to benefit from the scourge of slavery. To do that, we are going to need all the help we can muster but, most of all, we are going to need help from white Americans. Therefore, our leaders must acquire a better understanding of our 'white kinfolk' *because they are the most powerful people on earth.* If they desire, they could totally free us; they have the power.

Why would white folk help slaves?

*H*istory reveals that without decent white folk, slaves would be still in chains; the lash would still be drawing blood from our backs.

Let us leave our prejudices behind for a moment. Let's look at our white kinfolk in a different, factual light and with an open mind. We know that much effort went into making slaves and maintaining slavery. Crimes against humanity were committed, and many people died just so we could arrive at this juncture. A war was fought on American soil that pitted white brother against brother, and white father against son and according to history, it was all because of us — American Slaves. Some praiseworthy white folk sacrificed their families and gave their lives for us, yet we don't want to acknowledge being who we are! Something has to be wrong with that reasoning!

> **"Our leaders are the ones who gave up."**

While our neglect was and still is a terrible thing, history has shown that not all whites were in opposition to American Slaves being free. And, let us not forget, there were many whites marching with descendants of slaves during our Civil Rights movement. They were ready to go the distance with us. Yes, whites were actually following slaves. Whites not only understand how to 'follow the leader,' they enjoy following a good leader.

Even though Dr. King pointed us in the right direction, those slave leaders who were left standing didn't know how to assume the reins. *Our leaders are the ones who gave up!*

It's time for us get on with the struggle, but this time we must follow Dr. King's directions. We will proceed to the economic battlefield and engage our forces in the business arena, but not in that order. I don't believe all whites would oppose the descendants of slaves advancing into the American mainstream. Many agree that we deserve to be well-represented in the American scheme of things. Astute whites say we are needed, and business minded whites would be receptive to our entrance if the proper incentives were put into place. They understand the enormous amount of profit that can be made off of the commercialization of American Slaves. And that's not bad at all — *this is business*; we want our white kinfolk to profit from our racial advancement, too. The more they profit, the more they will help us — that's what American business is all about. That's what the concept 'good ol' boys' is all about! How do I know this? I used to be a good ol' boy.

Separate — yet bound together

After the war, most whites mentally dismissed us except to wish they had us back in the harness providing cheap labor. Whites' major concern was slaves stealing from them to survive or an angry slave starting a "nigger uprising." However, as time passed, slaves proved to be a peace-loving people. Slave uprisings have been few and far between, and always provoked. Still, some whites kept right on doing terrible things to our people. Therefore, peacefully coexisting amidst discrimination, injustice, and violence is an art that American Slaves were forced to perfect in order to survive in our hostile environment.

Underlying resentment causes slaves to *unconsciously* think whites conspire against our people, and even that they dutifully follow some strict rules of hate. Before I went into business,

I, too, thought whites were 'in cahoots' with the clandestine, hooded mistreatment of our people. However, after being in business for a while, I found out that there is no conspiracy that all whites follow.

The idea that whites work together, like ants or bees contributing to the common good to do what's best for whites, or that they follow some secret rules for the betterment of "whitedom" is a mistaken fantasy. The majority of whites do what's best for them, individually. True, there are some whites who hate the descendants of slaves, and sometimes they negatively influence other whites, but not all whites are so easily influenced by hate brought on by ignorance. All population groups have their share of good and evil. Yes, whites can be scheming, manipulative, conniving, ruthless, and outright evil at times, but it is an individual choice, not some "white man's way." But there is one thing that we must be aware of: Whites will act in 'violent concert' when they even *think* the safety of our country is threatened. When we add common sense to what little is known about American Slaves, it is clear to see that, unlike some other nationalities, American Slaves have never been a threat to our country, or to white people. Even in expressing our deep anguish and desperation during the riots, *it was our own neighborhoods that we burned!* ❖

> *"The majority of whites do what's best for them, individually. True, there are some whites who hate the descendants of slaves, and sometimes they negatively influence other whites, but not all whites are so easily influenced by hate brought on by ignorance."*

CHAPTER 25

Ghettonomics in the Suburbs

(An American Slave receives a doctorate)

Modern day slaves don't care to admit that we are treated differently from other nationalities because the average of us don't understand why. Consequently, most of us never deal with our maltreatment until there is a race-related flare-up. It wasn't until I moved to the suburbs that I thought seriously enough about my people, or my being a part of a 'different people,' to actually make discriminating evaluations.

"When greedy whites take unfair advantage of ignorant slaves in the world of commerce, they hinder all descendants of slaves from legitimately competing in the American business arena."

When I compared our two people I became aware that, because of color discrimination, a free-minded white person and a slave with a slave mentality can look at the same set of circumstances but envision two entirely different endings to that same situation, simply because our two people are treated so differently. This applies even more so in the business arena.

It was whites who advised me to move to the suburbs.

They advised that, in my position, it was best for me to be around upscale businesspeople. After I was there for a while, they further advised I also needed to upgrade my lifestyle socially; that I needed to associate with people in my class. When I did just that, I found myself surrounded by intelligent, white businesspeople. I was now a certified minority businessman and I had the necessary documentation to confirm it. I had finally arrived *or so I thought.* What I found out is that commercial bigotry is negatively impacting American Slaves' overall population.

The suburbs and my old 'hood are two entirely different worlds. The way I see America's racial situation now is not the way I used to see it. By moving away and then back again, I gained an entirely new perspective. The 'hood to me now is what the "Final Frontier" is to "Star Trek." I see only raw talent and untainted possibilities.

After being around the whites who had maneuvered me from my inherited ghetto life to my newly acquired upper class, suburban life, it became increasingly clear to me that to them I was just an ignorant minority, a commodity to be used and put on display when necessary.

Whenever the real movers and shakers needed a minority, the whites who had programmed me to be their modern day slave would bring me out. Now, there is nothing wrong with being important enough to be of use to those who are in control of America's wealth. It's what most smart business people, worldwide, work toward most of their lives in order to place themselves in a position of influence and instrumentality. However, the other side of the 'use' coin is 'misuse.' To be used properly in an industrial arena, one must know who the players are, what game is being played, one's own role in the game, and the reward for playing the game. Ultimately, people expect to be rewarded for their effort.

Being a descendant of slaves, and being used in ignorance as a minority because I wasn't certain of my own identity, is not only misusing me, it's misusing my people. That's where a 'true slave' *should* draw the line.

"A free-minded white person, and a slave with a slave mentality can look at the same set of circumstances, but envision two entirely different endings to that same situation, simply because our two people are treated so differently."

When greedy whites take unfair advantage of ignorant slaves in the world of commerce, they hinder all descendants of slaves from legitimately competing in the American business arena. When ignorant slave leaders let others take advantage of them in any situation, it uses up our people's chances of sharing in the American dream. Unfortunately, the fact is slaves are easily taken advantage of. In the upper echelon of business the typical slave is uninformed due to the lack of experience, and whites know this. To put it bluntly, most of the time we don't really know what we are doing at this higher level, but whites do know. More important, slaves have scant avenues available through which we can obtain this information. This puts us at the mercy of those unscrupulous whites who roam the brutal business arena looking for easy prey. How do I know this? After I learned the game, and whites were sure of my loyalty to the 'game,' I was invited to accompany them on their 'hunts.'

Some of these whites would like to help our people, but the average white businessperson knows that the only way descendants of slaves can be helped is through business. That's a problem because whites rely on statistics according to the rule of 'solvency.' These businessmen, because of their white business mentalities, have no other choice but to consider slaves worthless and slave businesses 'fair game.' When an astute businessman steps back and views American Slaves overall — no matter their pedigree — *that's what they think they see.* Thus far, we are a scattered, nonproductive people without a leader or a mission.

Once I had a chance to digest my new surroundings it wasn't hard summing up the suburbs, the manufacturing arena, and the 'hood, in regards to our people. Most ordinary descendants of slaves are openly treated as if they are damaged goods left over from slavery. It was even easier summing up the political arena. Slave leaders are thought of as Uncle Toms, especially by whites, because they have allowed our masses to be abused by those in positions of authority. *There was a time that these abusers were all white.*

Once I added reflection to my newly acquired insight, my frustrations overcame me — I couldn't take it anymore! Consequently, I did a terrible thing — I broke the code of "slavery silence." From the beginning of slavery, there has been a code of silence between our two peoples. Neither will tell the other group what they truly feel or what their thoughts are racially. During slavery whites didn't want our foreparents to know the truth and, if a slave were to speak the truth, it could cost him his life. Nowadays, no one pays too much attention to the truth about racial issues because the real truth is being covered up, and slave truth is usually blurted out in a fit of anger.

Fortunately, the experience of being in business taught me to curb my anger and, besides that, I really liked these white fellows. They might have been taking advantage of me but, at the same time, they were helping me. I was learning from them that proper education is extremely costly, especially the type of edification not taught in school. Realizing my identity and knowing that American Slaves are a brand new people, I could live with whites taking advantage of me personally because all I could see was great potential and a bright future for all descendants of slaves — if only I could learn enough.

When I thought the time was right I called a private meeting and painstakingly described my feelings to my white friends. To my surprise, they didn't get upset; they said my racial synopsis made sense. Telling them the truth about how I felt about America, myself and them, and what I could see up ahead for all of America, removed some of the ignorance these whites had exhibited concerning the descendants of slaves. I was candid and straight to the point. I didn't even concern myself over the possibility they would cancel lucrative contracts they had with my company.

Even when I thought I was well off, financially, I reasoned that my measly trappings were nothing compared to what my people could have if I could accept being myself, put my feelings aside, and let these white businessmen teach me to be the best that I could be. Perhaps then I could teach other slaves to be the best they could be. To me, this made sense.

Finding help in the suburbs

Unlike our Uncle Tom leaders I didn't move to the suburbs trying to get away from my people, or to have a good time; I was there on business. Living in the suburbs, and then coming to fully understand my identity, didn't make me docile or subservient like one might think, or like slaves were made to behave during slavery. Quite the opposite, the suburbs taught me to curb my anger and how to conduct myself to get what I want out of situations (the same as whites). In my new community, I became aware of who and what I was dealing with, what I was competing for, and with whom I was competing. This upper-class environment demanded that my concentration become a lot sharper. I had to focus, and when I did I actually came face to face with myself. I saw who I really am.

Not being a cohesive unit, descendants of slaves aren't a 'focused' people. In the ghetto I never thought about success. Most descendants of slaves figure: What's the use? People like us almost always come up on the short end of the stick or get dumped on, anyway. The typical slave doesn't center his attention on being a successful competitor in the American scheme of things because slaves don't seriously compete. We survive, though that certainly is a form of competing, but at a much lower level. American Slaves still compete for the crumbs that fall from others' tables but, because of our inherited racial unawareness, descendants of slaves don't realize this.

Successful 'non-communication'

For more than a hundred years, ignorant white leaders haven't allowed sensible discussion about slavery and, for that same amount of time, slave leaders have been afraid to demand justice. History has shown that whenever a slave demanded justice he was again putting his life on the line. Whites don't want slaves to be heard from at all, much less demand justice. However, at some point in time, our leaders are either going to have to lead, follow, or get the hell out of the way. They must start developing a dialogue with whites about our people. There is no communication between our two cultures in regards to slavery. It's as if we are all waiting to see what is going to happen, which is inexcusable. As Confucius is credited with saying: "A man who has committed a mistake and doesn't correct it is committing another mistake."

Now that I look back I can understand at least why straightforward communication is difficult between our two people. There was a time when, because of my ignorance, I wouldn't allow a white person to talk to me truthfully about my people, especially about us being slaves or being ignorant from the roots up. It would have hurt my feelings. However, when I moved to the suburbs I began to recognize the vast deficiency among my people. It became important that I acquire as much "un-talked-about" knowledge as I could. I knew it would assist me in helping my people. I arrived at the conclusion it's what descendants of slaves *don't* talk about that we *need* to talk about. It was in the suburbs that I came to understand the impact of the word ignorant. I found out that *ignorance* is the main supporter of second-class citizenship.

Realizing that it was whites who forced this ignorance upon our foreparents, and then believing whites were in cahoots together *against my people*, hindered my talking about slavery. But after I got the ball rolling, whites were going out of their way to enlighten me — *a descendant of slaves!*

It was a white person who told me there is honor in being an American Slave, much more than in being an American white. He said that, as a people our 'hands are clean,' and by our nation starting anew we have the opportunity to construct our racial plan so our group will remain uncontaminated. Then he really surprised me. He said the rectification of slavery to black America's satisfaction would cleanse the hands of whites.

Once I adjusted to the suburbs and my wariness faded, the thirst for true knowledge was recognized. I could now draw from my white brothers for my personal benefit then (after a while), even for my people's benefit. A white person who helps a descendant of slaves is a friend, but when this same person puts forth effort to help the slave's racial group when he doesn't have to the slave not only has a true friend he has at last reunited with his white brethren who, heretofore, were also lost in handed-down ignorance.❖

CHAPTER 26

Second-Class Leadership
(Results in second-class citizenship)

During slavery, slaves were programmed to believe they were little more than animals; since then we have been gradually elevated, but only to second-class citizens. We have endured this status and the concomitant maltreatment with grumbling, but without significant unified protest. The world mistakes our silence for consent; therefore, other American racial groups perceive us as second-class.

If another group were to state openly that we are second-class citizens, or that we are ignorant slaves, it would upset us terribly. Our leaders would grab their bullhorns, organize a protest rally, and proclaim their outrage in carefully worded and succinct statements to produce 'sound bites' for the TV news cameras. The hastily gathered crowd of usual suspects would be throwing a veritable conniption fit, but in vain because whoever says we are second-class citizens is telling the truth.

Descendants of slaves being discriminated against is a byproduct of our being

"'African American' leaders shun the whole truth surrounding slavery because they know that this particular truth, served whole, makes average whites apprehensive."

second-class citizens. Racial ignorance makes us susceptible to this negative condition and our second-rate status. A group of gullible people who are being led by uninformed leaders into the brutal, business arena *without any type of success plan* couldn't help but be regarded as second-class citizens!

The tragedy of the racial situation in America is twofold: Slave descendants who call themselves our leaders don't talk intelligently to their white counterparts about the maltreatment descendants of slaves receive. They are afraid of repercussions. Therefore, when it comes to slavery, their argument is reduced to doubletalk they believe is acceptable to whites. Secondly, those few slave leaders who are not frightened of whites are nonetheless wary of their fellow descendants of slaves. They dare not publicly point at defects our community of people may have because we don't take racial criticism very well — even from our own. Most of us are reflexively ill at ease about the topic of slavery. Many among us would mistake constructive criticism about our brethren for racial slander. Calling descendants of slaves "slaves," out in the open, could cause a slave uprising.

Our leaders know that most slaves individually would rather look good temporarily than hear the awful truth about their person openly, *especially if that truth says we are ignorant slaves.* This gives lazy, nonthinking leaders the perfect excuse they need for not doing their jobs, which is telling their followers the whole truth even when it hurts.

'African American' leaders shun the whole truth surrounding slavery because they know that this particular truth, served whole, makes average whites apprehensive. This is another example of our weak, ignorant leadership. Our leaders' stifling the truth of slavery helps keep slavery covered up. The truth of slavery shouldn't cause the descendants of slaves to feel uneasy. It should make us realize that help is imminent.

Our so-called leaders have always been the gate-keeper who

filter the information slaves receive. Their job should be to get accurate information to us, not just the information that sounds politically correct. Sure, the bulk of us are not that educated, but many of us do have enough 'mother wit' to figure out the purpose of information that is accidentally 'leaked.' Our leaders rarely think about purpose. They usually make a quick decision to attack distasteful information or elect to "kill the messenger" before our people get the message!

"Our leaders know that most slaves, individually, would rather look good, temporarily, than hear the awful truth about their person, openly — especially if that truth says we are ignorant."

Consider this: Paul Hornung is a member of the Football Hall of Fame. The 1956 Heisman Trophy winner he went on to become a star for the Green Bay Packers. In 2004, he said regarding his college alma mater, the University of Notre Dame, "We can't stay as strict as we are as far as the academic structure is concerned because we've got to get the black athlete. We gotta get the black athlete," he commented on a radio broadcast. "We must get the black athlete if we are going to compete." Mr. Hornung was immediately attacked, chastised, made to apologize, and then he was hushed up.

Why was Mr. Hornung attacked? Did he accidentally leak vital information? After thinking about his statement, I concluded that what Mr. Hornung said is true. And it's only fair that standards be 'adjusted' in areas where we have been disadvantaged. It's the only way we can catch up. Hornung has been attacked for stating publicly what should be obvious to all.

If the shoe fits — wear it!

*D*r. King made it clear that the only way our people's bottom line can be secured is on the economic battlefield, *through business.* I believe our leaders have missed that message, also. Judging from their actions they just don't understand the significance of Dr. King's wisdom.

Following are some words (my italics) taken from the front of Dr. Martin L. King's book: *Why We Can't Wait:*

> "Rev. Jackson is the founder and president of the Rainbow/PUSH Coalition, an organization committed to fighting for social, political and economic justice for *all people of all races, genders and creeds.* Rev. Jackson is also renowned for his *efforts around the world* to spread the promise of democracy, human rights and peace."

Reverend Jackson is continually in the racial spotlight, and he is singled out as being our leader; therefore, his organization and his name get a preponderance of attention. Nonetheless, if our leaders direct organizations committed to fighting for social, political, and economic justice for *all people of all races, genders, and creeds,* their efforts are too all-encompassing to do much for anyone. *American Slaves must be singled out — not mingled in!* We need and deserve undiluted attention!

Descendants of slaves should be aware — only our racial leaders have the capabilities, connections, and the authority to seek out and acquire help for our collective benefit. Only a single-minded leader will be committed enough to lead us in the economic arena.

We must find us another unifying leader — a worthy succes-

Too often, our would-be leaders 'breeze in' from far away just long enough to deliver their 'canned' speeches at staged events. They cast about big words in verbose language that most ordinary slaves don't understand.

---

sor to Dr. King. We can ill afford to wait! There's been a leadership vacuum since April 4, 1968! We need someone to rally, rouse and revive us. We need a charismatic, noble, single goal-oriented leader — not self-serving connivers.

"Only a single-minded leader will be committed enough to lead us in the economic arena."

There's a reason the United States has one President, not a panel of peers. We need focus and unity of purpose, not the divisiveness of competing self-anointed leaders. I firmly believe America would support proper reparations for slavery that was perpetrated in America, but only if we elect a chief executive of the slave nation to represent us all. ❖

CHAPTER 27

Reparations Versus Welfare

(World-class surplus)

Proper reparations for slavery could wipe out welfare as we know it. However, we must understand welfare and 'racial reparations' and how to best benefit from the latter. If restitution for slavery were to happen, it would still take an ample amount of time to eradicate welfare because of the amount of special education needed and the time needed to educate. First off, there should be neither free money nor free rides for slaves. Welfare-minded slaves will definitely oppose that because too many of us think we are owed both.

Some will ask: If funds awarded, or contributed, to our slave nation are not divided up evenly, how will slaves on the bottom benefit? Simple: Capitalism works! Those slaves who are busi-

> *"Slave businesspersons who benefit from the slave program would be duty-bound and legally compelled to help elevate the lowest of the descendants of American Slaves who are on welfare and those on the poverty level to be eligible to stay in the program."*

nesspersons can be designated to participate in our advancement plan as our pioneers. They would lead the way because they have the ability to create jobs as their business grows. Once such enterprises are adopted by major corporations, management would be obligated to adopt a neighborhood, or assist in the upgrading of targeted inner-city streets and neighborhoods. They would mentor less fortunate slaves who can someday participate in the plan as trained leaders and prospective role models. They would be given explicit directions and instructions, along with desired expectations, all of which would be closely monitored, properly documented, and then made public.

Slave businesspersons who benefit from the slave program would be duty-bound and legally compelled to help elevate the lowest of the descendants of American Slaves who are on welfare, and those on the poverty level, to be eligible to stay in the program. This would shift the burden of responsibility for our slave nation into view. We would finally know who is responsible for our well-being.

To get the show on the road, it's vital that slaves who are businesspersons *voluntarily* step forward when they get the word. We cannot put this off until tomorrow. We must combine our minds in a timely fashion, and we must 'strike while the iron is hot.'

In rarely held open and frank discussions, whites make it clear they think our business leaders are slow-witted because we keep waiting for our government to think up programs beneficial to our ethnic group. Business-minded leaders are the key link missing in our advancement. We don't have a financially stable upper class that balances out the country's wealth in proportion to our country's ethnic head count, and we never will unless slaves, who are businesspeople, take it upon themselves to unite.

Businesspersons at the top of our slave nation have always

been stifled. They have never been in a position financially to start the 'trickle-down' that would offset welfare and positively affect our people to ensure more prosperity for each individual in our group. This is another aftereffect from slavery. Commerce was left out of our programmed approach to life. The master didn't want slaves to *have* his wealth — they were his wealth!

Welfare programs breed welfare-mindedness

There are welfare programs for individuals who can't help themselves or have fallen upon hard times, and *thank goodness for welfare programs!* The average slave couldn't have made it this far without some form of assistance. However, keep in mind these programs are designed to assist individuals only and should not be abused by an ethnic group that should be competing with other groups in the human race, the American market, and in the world market. For our people to progress, we need as many of our people as possible to be productive, not impoverished.

Our leaders hear and read the unemployment statistics. This report tells them that our people are the most underemployed. Yet, our people were bred for one reason — to work! American Slaves should be one hundred percent employed; that was the sole purpose of our being. That's why we are here!

There are too many descendants of slaves on welfare who don't belong there. Welfare-minded slaves soon lose the assertiveness it takes to compete in the human race and in American life. Those slaves who are defrauding our government go after and receive assistance simply because they know how to get it. Our leaders have never told them that association brings about assimilation or, to quote a white folks' expression, "You are what you eat."

If slaves had a plan and merely were using welfare as a *temporary* stepping stone to get into a better position, I could understand this. However, too many slaves collecting welfare are swindlers; they don't have a plan past bilking our government. Before they know it, receiving undue benefits becomes habit. They pass this bad habit on to their offspring, eventually making welfare a permanent attachment to many of our people by association.

Because our slave nation doesn't have a plan that includes all of us, many seem doomed to becoming welfare recipients. The average descendant of slaves is already ignorant, but when we get infected with petty greed we get caught up in what we *think* is free money. This 'free money' is causing many to waste their lives in abject poverty.

To stop this welfare travesty, descendants of slaves must draft a leader who understands that a person cannot beg one's way to wealth. Welfare is a disincentive to descendants of slaves. Our leader must help us understand that no community of people can beg, borrow, or steal their way out of poverty. People who have been deprived must be told this in a language they can understand. They must be given a starting point and primary direction they can follow. The slave nation must be taught how to plan for the long haul. Those who teach us must understand how to communicate a racial advancement plan to those who are unsophisticated.

Since integration, down-to-earth talk seems to be beneath our highfalutin leaders. Most of the time they are embarrassed at the way most of us talk. They fail to realize that we are a young, new people. We are just now in the midst of learning language and communication. Our slang dialect is evidence of our identity; we inherited it from slavery. When African American leaders do talk to us they try to hide their slavery slang. They cast about big words in verbose language that most ordinary slaves don't understand. They very seldom use plain talk that slaves can identify with. This only broadens our communication gap.

Entertainer Bill Cosby, a well-to-do black was on the right track when he criticized descendants of slaves on the Tavis Smiley, PBS TV talk show. Mr. Cosby said, "Blacks are not parenting their children," and that Black youth especially "need to speak standard language."

"Our leader must make us understand that no community of people can beg, borrow, or steal their way out of poverty. People who have been deprived must be told this in a language each can understand, and they must be given a starting point and primary direction they can follow."

I will agree with some of what Bill said. In an industrial society proper grammar, according to whom the speaker is communicating with, is vitally important. However, Mr. Cosby forgot about slavery and who we are. This is another case of our leaders not knowing how to help us because they don't know our true identity. Could it be that Bill hasn't matured to the point that he realizes slaves are an adolescent people? Maybe he doesn't understand that our nation is just now learning *how* to "speak standard language."

During slavery, talking like the master denoted intelligence, and that was a *dangerous* no-no. Mr. Cosby is a wise man. I would think he could understand why some of us talk the way we do.

African American leaders have removed themselves too far from the lowest of us. They can no longer tell us the value of "earning our daily bread by the sweat of our brow" in words that are motivational. It's true that those who aren't collecting some type of subsidy typically work for minimum wage, but we should not let this discourage us to the point that we cease struggling to be productive. Help is just around the corner; let us try to be ready when it gets here. Racial production will wipe out racial welfare. Let us not forget our ancestors were American Slaves; slaves were bred to labor long and hard. We are the descendants of those hard workers! If we learn to pull together we can work our way out of poverty.

Weak leadership has allowed slaves to become hardened to the humiliation that stems from standing in a welfare line and having another slave parcel out *undue* aid. African American leaders appear blind to the shame and pity that connects itself to those of their followers who have sunk so low they are barely able to survive in a 'free society' while others around them, especially their leaders, are thriving.

American Slaves shouldn't be deceived into relying upon welfare. Receiving welfare is not a step up in life — quite the opposite. Welfare was designed to help individuals who are in such dreadful condition they can't help themselves. We descendants of slaves could help ourselves if intelligent leaders provided us with proper direction. We haven't fallen on hard times, and neither should we fear hard times. Slaves were born into slavery. Our ancestry took root *right in the middle of hard times!*

The average slave has no appreciation of the complexities of the business arena, but the masses of us understand most every twist and turn of the 'lower end' of the welfare game. We know how much, where it's at, what it takes to get it, who is getting it, how they got it, and how long they are going to continue getting it before they get caught by those who 'police' the game. The rules of the business and welfare games are similarly intricate, but American Slaves are *playing in the wrong game.*

The trickle-down from improper, racial leadership leads to inappropriate guidance in our inner cities. Without guidance, young slaves are prone to picking up bad habits too easily. American Slaves don't need welfare in the form of charity; it creates a welfare mentality. We need a special help program that addresses the overall interests of our people and opposes welfare in the form of charity.

> *"Whites used discrimination to cause our condition.*
>
> *It is only fair and honorable that discrimination be used to repair the damage it caused to so many fellow human beings."*

Some might say: If America helps the descendants of American Slaves with a special help program, it's discrimination. Well, it was discrimination and other evils done against slaves that caused us to be so far behind. We need special help. Whites used discrimination to cause our condition. It is only fair and *honorable* that discrimination be used to repair the damage it caused to so many fellow human beings.

Our leaders are afraid to proclaim openly that descendants of slaves need special help. They say it casts us as 'being different.' Well, I'm here to tell them we *are different! We have a unique pedigree. We are descended from slaves.* We are descended from selectively bred Americans! ❖

CHAPTER 28

Was Dr. King's Dream Realized?

(Pride, oh pride — where art thou?)

American Slaves' finest hour was when we were following Dr. King. He knew how to lead us toward freedom. The integration battles he orchestrated are a vital part of our racial foundation. Given direction, we marched. Offered hope, we strived. Shown injustice, we protested. He spoke, we listened. Powerfully led, we eagerly followed. We didn't understand who we were, but we were searching, and we knew we were on the right road because we could 'feel it.' We knew we were on the same page because we were highly motivated, hand in hand, singing loudly, and marching toward freedom.

Even though slaves were programmed to fear the master because of his brutality, this was the only time in our short history that we openly

> "Even in death Dr. King was trying to show us the way to freedom. His final exit clearly showed us who we are as a people: His remains were carried to his final resting place by mules pulling a wagon."

demonstrated against oppression as a people, and some slaves were actually willing to die for our people's freedom.

Even in death, Dr. King was trying to show us the way to freedom. His final exit clearly showed us who we are as a people: His remains were carried to his final resting place by mules pulling a wagon — not by a Cadillac hearse, nor beautiful, high-spirited horses pulling a regal, white carriage. Most Americans felt his funeral was an orchestrated portrayal of a slave who has "laid down his heavy burden, and is going home," and they were right. However, because slaves have forgotten so much about slavery, we didn't realize the real significance of such a humble procession.

Having mules pulling the wagon that carried Dr. King's coffin was a visible, wake-up indicator that slave leaders should have studied. It's true this was how slaves of old were carried to the burial ground, but why in this day and time? My interpretation: It signified he, too, was an American Slave — an American who knew his heritage, and this soil is his home!

Nothing has happened since Dr. King's death that would change this. We have always been, we still are, and always will be, *descendants of American Slaves!*

The journey continues

If following Dr. King in life and then accompanying his mule-drawn remains to his final resting place was our finest hour, and he was leading us toward freedom, isn't that what we should still be doing — seeking our freedom to the finish? That's what our greatest leader was doing. Our leader was slain, but I figured someone would pick up the banner and continue in his footsteps. Who could have known that Dr. King's act would be so hard to follow? Now that I reflect back, we did try to persevere, but we didn't follow the path Dr. King was traveling. We followed ignorant leaders who were lost. They took an errant turn, and since then we have been aimless. What little unity we had quickly dissipated.

It's clear to see that when the Negroes of King's day adopted a new, fallacious 'African American' identity, this development didn't alleviate our problems. Slave descendants are still being discriminated against and abused. Losing our way and changing our identity just elevated a few Uncle Toms and swept our crisis under the rug.

> *"Integration was a major human rights victory, a battle at the masses level that we should never belittle, but integration was just one of many battles the descendants of American Slaves must fight, if we wish to be truly free."*

Integration was a major human rights victory, a battle at the masses' level that we should never belittle. However, integration is just one of many battles the descendants of American Slaves must fight if we wish to be truly free.

Integration allowed the masses of slaves a degree of access to public facilities. Our elite were allowed admittance into white neighborhoods to live and function among whites. At the first sign of integration, our leaders left us behind. If they had been leaving us to gain a tactical advantage that would benefit our people, instead of them trying to get away *from* us, they would have been praised instead of despised. If our leaders could see the entire picture, they would see that integration removed our elite from among our masses, integrated them with whites, and then mentally relocated them to the suburbs. This was a side effect from integration that only added to our racial division.

Here are questions all slaves should ask themselves:

❶ Was Dr. King's dream of freedom for all fulfilled?

❷ Did Dr. King's dream extend past integration and, if so, what was it?

❸ Did the perpetrators, with one bullet, achieve their mission and stop the American Slaves nation from organizing and then advancing into the American mainstream?

❹ What happened to make us suddenly change our direction and our racial name?

❺ Did Dr. King change our name from Negro to African American and, if he did, for what reason — and if he didn't, who did, and why?

❻ Who will be next to take up the gauntlet and have the intelligence, yet be unafraid, to point toward freedom?

❼ Did Dr. King leave a continuation plan other than telling us that our next battle would be fought on the economic battlefield and, if he did, where is it, what is it, and which of his lieutenants was next in line to implement it?

❽ While Dr. King was alive we were Negroes and he was trying to lead us to freedom. After he was assassinated we became first — Blacks, then African Americans. What purpose did it serve?

Reading between the lines

Dr. King couldn't predict steps to take for each upcoming, unknown situation we would encounter because the road that American Slaves must travel is unique. However, he did suggest different measures which could be applied if future situations happened to be similar to those he had already faced.

He told us what is about to happen in America, and then he told us what *must* happen up ahead for us to keep on the road toward freedom. It's up to our leaders to figure what specific advances should be made, and then plan our strategies from the tactical information Dr. King used in similar circumstances.

When Dr. King was jailed in Birmingham, he constructed a letter that highlighted the division among our people by illustrating the division between him and other clergymen who didn't understand what he was doing at that time. Then he went on to explain how he suppressed this divisiveness in order that he and other ministers could work together and, through their collective, unified efforts, achieve victory. Now keep in mind this was the state of slave leadership at that time. It appears those slaves who became leaders didn't learn a thing from Dr. King. They went out and got themselves anointed African Americans. This just added another division to all of the other divisive names that keeps us a divided people.

> *African American leaders of today are even more divided than Dr. King and those ministers were then.*

African American leaders of today are even more divided than Dr. King and those ministers were then. Our people are more divided now than we were when we thought we were Negroes.

Dr. King was teaching us the bare basics of business, and how to overcome our internal divisiveness, in case something happened to him. While outlining his moves, Dr. King's plan was by no means spelled out. Even so, a perceptive leader should have figured it out. He told us plainly where the next battle would be waged — on the economic battlefield.

Dr. King ended his book by telling us that we must remain nonviolent, and that our nonviolent strategy should benefit *all mankind.*

Our "leaders" have some explaining to do

The hurt created by slavery was underscored by riots when Dr. King was eliminated from our lives. We burned our own neighborhoods as a public scream of despair; we didn't know what else to do. We had no leadership to direct us. Our residual leadership had "flown the coop." We were a hurt people crying out in anguish, expressing our pain. However, the opportunistic looters got the preponderance of the press coverage.

Instead of the riots making an everlasting statement that would benefit our ethnic community, they were short-lived, and the flames were soon extinguished, causing our protestation to be in vain. The news media made us look like scoundrels, instead of focusing on the criminals, the real villains, who killed Dr. King.

The riots should have been a wake-up call for our residual leadership to come up with a continuation plan. Regrettably, this didn't happen.

After the riots, the descendants of slaves stood by helplessly and watched as other racial groups migrated into our neighborhoods and took over the abandoned buildings that had only recently housed thriving businesses. We didn't realize what we were witnessing and neither did our leaders, because slaves have never been taught to think commercially. We were just glad to see stores opening up again in our vicinity so we could buy bare necessities. Immigrants wresting control of our neighborhood economy never entered our minds.

Writing about the truth in America has always been a delicate undertaking and, because of doubletalk and misconception, writing about slavery in America and how the descendants of slaves truthfully feel about America is unheard of. This is because of shame and fear, which brings us to another obstacle. How can we help American Slaves, as a group, if we don't talk about race, or race relations, or if we are afraid to write what

"The hurt created by slavery was underscored by riots when Dr. King was eliminated from our lives. We burned our own neighborhoods as a public scream of despair; we didn't know what else to do."

every descendant of slaves feels but doesn't understand?

When I was child, the Second World War rumbled to a close. There were Jewish businesses on many corners in slave neighborhoods. When Dr. King was assassinated, the descendants of slaves impulsively burned out those neighborhood businesses because we always considered these people foreigners. We still don't understand immigration, commerce, or America because now foreigners from all countries are coming to America, seeking the America dream. Some of them come straight to our neighborhoods to get their start, and then they move up. America should have taught her slaves how to work their way up from the bottom long ago.

Those who claim they are leading our people still don't understand descendants of slaves should have come into possession of those commercial buildings. They are constantly talking about improving slave neighborhoods, but that's all it is — talk. They have yet to see that businesses in slave neighborhoods should be predominantly owned by our people. I wonder have they reflected that our "buy black" campaign could have been a success if our people had come into possession of those businesses. If this had been the case, we could *buy black* because those from within our own people would be able to "sell black."

During a private discussion, a perturbed mother told me that her daughter worked for a foreigner who owned a store in her neighborhood. It seems the merchant paid the young woman two hundred dollars to marry his nephew in order that his nephew could come to American and become a citizen. However, this outrage was not the mother's primary complaint. The mother was upset because, subsequent to the marriage, her daughter had to work for 50 dollars a week instead of the agreed upon minimum wage. Her hours were increased to 80 per week instead of the 40 that she previously worked. Now that the girl was married, according to her husband's custom, she no longer had a say in her own life because she had to adhere to the rules of a foreign culture. The worst of the situation was that the young woman no longer made enough money to support her young son who her mother was obliged to keep. This type of exploitation of our people sounds too close to slavery to me. Destitution and abuse because of ignorance is commonplace in our inner cities.

When we look closely, we see that foreigners owning businesses in slave neighborhoods and taking advantage of our people is only part of our problem. Even if slaves tried to purchase commercial businesses in our neighborhoods, in most cases we can't come up with the necessary funds because of the dire condition we inherited from slavery.

If slaves did own the businesses in our neighborhoods and tried to borrow monies to expand commercially, we would run into stumbling blocks. An obvious weakness is that most slaves don't understand how to construct a business plan properly because the average slave doesn't understand business.

It will take shrewd business minds to teach slave leaders how to think on their feet, or how to take advantage of spontaneous situations. It will take persuasive slave leaders with sales ingenuity to explain to whites that sometimes they must put aside their greed and be generous to those to whom they owe so much. It is up to those who lead us to show whites how to be humane to our people and explain the benefits of being generous, as well.

> *"When we look closely, we see that foreigners owning businesses in slave neighborhoods and taking advantage of our people is only part of our problem. Even if slaves tried to purchase commercial businesses in our neighborhoods, in most cases, we can't come up with the necessary funds because of the dire condition we inherited from slavery."*

Seems our leaders would have learned something from the riots of April 1968, but they haven't. They still don't know how to react to today's racial incidents, not in a way that breeds commercial benefits for our people. Their mentality, which was handed down to them from other slaves, is to concur with the master. Our leaders don't realize they depend on whites to think for them. When our leaders do try to think, out of habit they are thinking for whites because they always think what is best for whites.

Not knowing they are slaves, our leaders wouldn't realize they have slave mentalities, or that they need to upgrade their way of thinking. After the riots died down, they waited in confusion until whites within the political system told them what to do that would end their uncertainty.

Once our unified leader is inaugurated and comprehends that slave mentalities do in fact still persist, he or she should also determine that if this state of mind is dealt with properly, it can be corrected.

Fear, the ultimate controller

*A*fter the grief-stricken chaos settled down following Dr. King's assassination, his frightened lieutenants split up. Being greedy, petty, small-minded, or afraid they could wind up in pine boxes some started their own separate groups, most of which were designated nonprofit corporations. Each sought to become a leader in his own way. Their shortsightedness facilitated the assassin's obvious goal of stopping our racial progress in its tracks.

Dr. King's legacy was to bring the descendants of slaves together in order that we could embark on our long trek toward freedom. It's shameful that Dr. King's assassin needed to slay only one person to stop all of us from marching toward freedom. If the civil rights cause had been close to completion, and if Dr. King's lieutenants had understood the plan, there would have been scant reason to assassinate Dr. King.

Is it possible that our leaders think our people are still moving forward? We are not moving forward; we are doing what slaves have always done — shuffling along behind the master at a safe distance. Our group stopped advancing the day our one leader was slain.

Some of those closest to Dr. King are still spinning their wheels trying to ferret out who may have conspired to slay him, instead of concentrating on pursuing his dream. Hindsight suggests that those responsible for slaying Dr. King must have known the ignorant condition of even his most trusted subordinates and understood that killing just him would stop us cold.

A number of those who marched with Dr. King have written books about the movement, purportedly recalling exactly what was said and what happened. Some are using Dr. King's name hoping to make a few bucks. Which of them has written about continuing the movement or about what steps must be taken next to advance our people?

> *"Dr. King's legacy was to bring the descendants of slaves together in order that we could embark on our long trek toward freedom. It's shameful that Dr. King's assassin needed to slay only one person to stop all of us from marching toward freedom."*

If we want to win the next battle in our quest for true freedom, which is the economic encounter that Dr. King alerted us to, we had better start preparing ourselves for commercial combat.

Some of Dr. King's followers are now published authors. A few have made efforts to help their people, but not in the area of commerce. They write about their personal experiences, thinking they are influencing our inner-city youths in a positive way. They need to think again because, first of all, these books won't help descendants of slaves on the economic battlefield. And, second, the influences couldn't help but be erroneous because most of these writers think they are 'African American' — and that's starting off wrong. The sooner our leaders accept the fact that we are descendants of slaves and not merely African Americans, the sooner they will begin to understand what influences the mentality of our people and what to do about it. ❖

CHAPTER 29

Back to the Pulpit
(Hallelujah — I'm saved, but am I free?)

Those descendants of American Slaves who are ministers need to reflect more carefully about their role in the slave community. They are influencing most of the descendants of slaves who show signs of having any mental strength left and, according to common perception, the clergy get their instructions straight from the Big Man Himself. Some religious leaders have set themselves up as a direct information link between God, His People, and the Promised Land — which makes them responsible for the spiritual side of our racial condition.

"There should be one 'root source' that all slaves can draw from for our betterment. This source must speak a factual language, without political doubletalk, in a fashion that slaves can, and will, heed.

In the near future, it will be necessary for our churches to take a more vigorous approach concerning the descendants of slaves' racial journey. How else will the masses of us ever hear that we have a chance at achieving the American dream?

It's the duty of the church to spread the word of freedom —

because churches have the ear of the flock. However, descendants of slaves who attend these religious institutions may never find out that their ancestors weren't properly freed from slavery. It might never cross their minds that they are America's only offspring. We have little chance of obtaining true freedom if the majority of us continue 'following the blind,' and they are not even *trying* to see.

The primary organizations in our ethnic population that are advancing are our churches. The only voices that many descendants of slaves heed are the voices of our ministers. While they are continually preaching, there is no clarity as to the damage done to our people. Even when there is racial unrest there is no clarity concerning our people, just confusion over individuals. Every now and then the clergy have been known to speak of the wrong done to 'black' people, but they don't have any solutions to offer.

Not one church in America stipulates that the American Slave nation is the main topic of the congregational teaching. We need to hear from the pulpits that we are slaves, and that, because we are slaves, we are America's first and only born group of people. To me these revelations are good news and should be shouted from the altar loud and clear. I have been preached at many times about the Jews and Gentiles and how these ethnic groups came about. It's mystifying that slave preachers are oblivious to our own genesis and how it came about.

Once ministers are made aware of their true identity, they should realize what their mission should be. They must put obtaining freedom and getting into heaven in their respective places. Preaching to 'wanna-be' African Americans about heaven and hell, and then rushing authentic American Slaves to the graveyard just so preachers can avoid fighting for freedom, is a ministerial cop-out. Churches are supposed to stand firm for what is right and take a solid, unyielding stand against what is wrong. *The enslavement of our people is wrong.*

I refuse to believe that the only way descendants of American Slaves can be free of white oppression, or be freed from the ignorant aftereffects of slavery, is by dying and going to our heavenly reward, or by impersonating Africans. I do believe that ministers are limiting God's supremacy simply because they don't know who they are. And if they don't know who they themselves are, it's a safe bet they don't know who they're leading. And if they don't know who they are leading, how could they possibly know what kind of help to ask God for in the first place?

Churches are the most notable institutions where the descendants of slaves gather for the purpose of receiving soul-saving information but, as of yet, American Slaves don't have a continuous communication system to receive important racial information. Most of the motivational messages we receive in church are about heaven and hell. We never get preached to about the abandonment or the lack of advancement of the descendants of slaves. We not only need to hear a language that all modern-day slaves can relate to, at our present stage and in our confused condition, we need to receive a straightforward, understandable message that gives specific directions for our entire nation. How else can we make decisions that could improve our lives? How else will we as a people know which way to go?

There should be one 'root source' that all slaves can draw from for our betterment. This source must speak a factual language, without political doubletalk, in a fashion that slaves can, *and will*, heed. Since our integration struggle, our leaders appear to think there is no reason for us to be together or communicate properly.

Recognizing the enemy

I was talking to a gathering of clergymen several of whom were claiming to be African Americans. When I disputed this and asked them to produce immigration papers, they became agitated.

At a neighborhood discussion, attorneys and politicians were claiming they too were African American. I asked them to produce immigration papers, but they couldn't either. They assumed

I was attacking them personally. Such leaders must stop assuming and start thinking. I wasn't attacking, and I wasn't trying to antagonize them. I was trying to help them accept the obvious — their heritage is all-American.

Our current leaders can't lead us to freedom if they think we are already free. They are not doing their jobs, which is a major reason why we are a divided, destitute people. They should realize we are America's only child. In such a thriving land we shouldn't be impoverished. Our division, coupled with our impoverished condition, puts pressure on our inner cities and our people.

I never understood that our people were so lacking in practicality and unity until I wanted to give back to my people. When I tried I came face to face with the question that has haunted American Slaves since slavery: *Who are we?* This prompted a question directed at me: Who am I really trying to help?

The search begins

In my search I untangled the myth that we are African Americans. It wasn't that hard to do; I just had to reflect on it. Consequently, I took a stab at helping American minorities. When I tried, however, my help was intercepted by all sorts of minority groups. Frustrated, I stopped trying to help minorities in general. I figured I would break rank and go straight to the source or, in slave language, "go to the 'root." I wound up at slavery.

After discerning I am still a slave, I decided to develop a way I could help our American Slave nation. I reasoned that it would be hard for evil forces to sidetrack or intercept this type of direct help. But first I decided to go through the 'proper channels.' Being militarily trained, I understand the necessity of strict discipline and strong, fair-minded leadership. I spoke to a close white friend who is a retired colonel in the military. He listened patiently and told me I was on the right track; that if he were in my shoes, he'd do exactly what I was considering. However, he did caution me to proceed carefully. He expounded on the dangers that have befallen those who have tried to help slaves in the past. He then offered his assistance if I should need it.

My friend's words were heartening; they lifted my spirit to the height I needed to make my next move. Having been raised in church, I understand the necessity of spiritual guidance before embarking upon an undertaking of this magnitude; therefore, I spoke to my minister. I told him that I was going to take it upon myself to help our people. He was overjoyed. He exclaimed, "Brother Shelton, the Lord's done laid his hands on you!" The light that leaped into his eyes was unequivocal. However, when I told him that, from my viewpoint, we are not African Americans but instead American Slaves, the mood and his attitude *both* changed. He was adamant he would not get involved with, or even *talk about,* slavery and definitely not about us being slaves now. He said, "Brother Shelton, let me tell you something and you listen carefully: Slavery has been over for better than a hundred years. Now, you oughta know better than to get mixed up in something like slavery. Haven't you been listening to my sermons about church members stirring up trouble? Man, slavery was terrible! Do you know how much distress something like what you are talking about could put on my flock? If I were to tell my tithing members they are slaves, the collection plate could turn up empty next Sunday. And if you go downtown messing with them white folks, talking about slavery and what they did to our foreparents, ain't nothing good gonna come from it."

> *"Our current leaders can't lead us to freedom, if they think we are already free."*

This is the person who was supposed to be guiding me. He said, "We are not slaves, Brother Shelton; I reason that we are 'colored' because of our different colors." That's when I knew I shouldn't be following this person another step.

Not only do some whites have a callous, backward mindset toward slavery, this is also the attitude of many of our own clergy who call themselves our leaders. Therefore this mindset reflects the accepted wisdom of our population in general because we are following these people.

Any preacher who doesn't want to hear the truth can't preach the truth. The truth is, slavery is not over, and can never be over until all slaves are truly freed. This should be the attitude of our ministers and, therefore, of our community.

I was talking to a well-known businessman who was once a high profile sports figure and role model. He had obviously "gotten religion" because he expressed to me how much money he contributed to the big, beautiful church they had just recently built. I told him I was trying to do my part to help fulfill the prophecy that Dr. King left to us; that I was trying to get our leaders together so they could start devising a financial help program to assist the descendants of slaves gaining admittance into the socioeconomic mainstream of America. He said the Bible teaches that people are not supposed to store up treasures here on earth. Now, here is a brother who has already made plenty of money, but he doesn't want other slaves to store up treasures. This is the attitude of a descendant of slaves who is really an Uncle Tom, but doesn't recognize it because he went out and purchased himself an ample amount of religion.

Another minister said I should "tone it down a little." He made it clear that I was speaking the truth too openly, and much too bluntly; that I should not be bringing slavery to the forefront of American life. I say slavery has been "toned down" far too long already. He should realize that racial friction has always been ongoing in America; it's our way of life. Doesn't he look at television? How can he not know that our people are still being brutalized? Doesn't he know that it's our young black men who are being gunned down in the streets!

If this minister were truly race conscious and had gained the necessary racial intelligence that would allow him to be called a leader, he would know I am trying to head off friction, not cause it. Can't he see where all of this violence which is caused by blatant discrimination, is leading?

Truth toned down isn't the whole truth. If it's not the whole truth, it's a lie!

I want all 'African American' ministers to understand that, if your flock consists largely of descendants of slaves, talking about slavery shouldn't be upsetting to your members, but be reassuring. Sure, slavery was distressing, but correcting the aftereffects of slavery shouldn't be offensive to the injured parties. We carry 'white-shame,' but we repress 'slave complaint.' The descendants of slaves are still trying to hide the abuse that whites did to our group while most of us are still living in poverty. We should be protesting to the whole wide world about what the white sector did (and is still doing to our people), but instead of screaming it from the rooftops we're hushing it up from the pulpits!

Religion and ignorance working in harmony

There is no place I'd rather be than in a lively house of worship. Church members shouting and singing emotionally is an exhilarating experience. I joined my church when I was 12 years old. After the Sunday sermon was over, the minister "opened the doors of the church." Those in attendance who wanted to go to Heaven were told to come forward and join.

I have been in the church most of my life. Now that I look back, I see that a great many slave churches have wealth. Yet, the church that I attended taught us that all rich people go straight to Hell, (though not in those exact words). During a Sunday sermon, the preacher told us that a rich man getting into heaven was as likely as a camel going through the eye of a needle. Like many others, I feared aspiring to riches. I reasoned that if I accumulated great wealth on this earth, I might wind up in Hell for eternity.

Since I have realized my identity, I've thought about that sermon in conjunction with slavery. I conclude that if the rich person is a descendant of slaves, and realizes it, and he knows the condition of his brethren and doesn't try to help us out of the misery that most of us live in, then he's an Uncle Tom. Maybe his going to Hell would be poetic justice. This especially applies to frightened slave preachers who are also greedy.

The slave masters knew that if slaves weren't called slaves, or if we weren't identified, or if the word slave was not used 'overtly' in regard to who we are, the slaves would eventually forget who they were. Before I talked to my preacher about helping my people, I had often wondered why the word slave is not used openly in black churches. When we look at history openly, we can't help but see that it was the slave master who taught slaves their religious beliefs in the first place. The master also realized the depth to which slaves believe in God; our people certainly didn't have anything else to believe in. He knew that if those slaves who were preachers could be kept racially uninformed, and if they taught their followers to maintain a spiritual attitude of meekness and humbleness and to accept poverty and abuse as a way of life, the childlike slaves would feel secure in knowing they would never have to face the fear that comes from pursuing freedom in a cruel white world. Just wait on the Lord! It's doubtful these preachers tell their congregations that, while we are waiting, we are losing the yearning for independence and the strength necessary to pursue true freedom.

I sincerely believe in God and, until lately, I tried to believe in our ministers, but after interviewing a few of then, I became disillusioned. If everybody procrastinates and then blames the Lord because we think He didn't come, not too much will ever get done. All this waiting is just another form of racial stagnation, especially when the Lord has already "made a way" by supplying us with this new information. As my father used to say, "The Lord's done done his part — now get your butt in gear and do yours."

If we descendants of American Slaves should ever get ourselves into full gear, our racial plan would come together in record time. Once it is in place, churches could be urged to work with businesses that are adopted by major corporations. Together, they could be obligated to adopt sections of a neighborhood, streets, or homes in targeted areas. Once slave churches and small businesses come together, the rest of our leaders will unite, too.

If those slaves who are businesspersons, educators, politicians, ministers, moonlighting-preachers, role models, or African American leaders don't want to hear the truth, aren't willing to tell the masses the truth, or can't take constructive criticism, then they are fearful of change or they have something to hide. In either case, they are worthless to the cause of freedom.

Eventually, we are all going to have to openly admit we have been blind to certain factors relating to slavery. One minister said my insight into slavery sounds revolutionary and suggested it might be too radical for the time period we are now living in. I reminded him that intelligent revolution and peaceful rebellion against injustice are honorable. American Slaves pursuing freedom in their own homeland shouldn't be considered disobedient or rebellious. We just want to be treated fairly.

It's the duty of our leaders to recognize the wrong done to our people, then they must have the nerve and passion to bring these ongoing injustices out into the open. When discrimination is exposed, it becomes every slave descendant's duty to stand firm against these injustices.

I refuse to follow a leader who accepts injustice. A true leader wouldn't continue to allow injustice to be dumped on his people simply because the dumping has been going on for our entire existence. Accepting injustice, and then covering up the offense, compounds the crime. American Slave descendants are innocent victims, and we unwittingly accept continuous racial abuse. Don't our leaders care? ❖

CHAPTER 30

"Nigger Rich!"

(The art of giving money away)

In street vernacular, 'nigger rich' is a term once used in the 'hood to identify upper-middle-class descendants of slaves. There have always been slaves considered nigger rich, but today some slaves are close to being 'white folks' rich. And some of them are kindhearted individuals who donate money to charities trying to help their people, but do they know where their money really goes? Not to the descendants of slaves. The difficulty of helping descendants of slaves is that there is no certified point where slaves receive direction or aid.

I have been neither nigger rich nor white folks rich, and I am definitely not an African American; however, there was a time I was most likely considered an Uncle Tom. Like some other descendants of slaves who are trying to help their people, I didn't realize it.

I'm quite sure there are

"Some whites have told me that they would like to lend a helping hand to descendants of slaves. However, whites have the same problem that slaves have: There is no central point where they can receive proper direction, support, or tax breaks as an incentive, if they did try to help."

many slaves out there who are trying to help their people, but don't have a clear understanding of exactly who they and their people are. Well, merely giving money to charity does little to help our people.

Some whites have told me that they would like to lend a helping hand to descendants of slaves. However, whites have the same problem that slaves have: There is no central point where they can receive proper direction, support, or tax breaks as an incentive, if they did try to help.

Some of our elite descendants of slaves give huge sums to oversized churches and white-owned charities. They must not fully understand the function of either. If they did, they would know charities don't hasten American Slaves' progress toward financial freedom, racial freedom, or any other kind of freedom. Churches typically point their members to heaven, not to earthly freedom.

Another sad truth is that when affluent slaves give to black colleges that don't teach the descendants of slaves who we are and how to help other slaves escape the racial poverty that slavery bred, they may get tax breaks for supporting education, but their donations only further American Slaves' ignorance. A race-conscious leader would realize that these monies are actually contributing to keeping the slave community in poverty. These funds retard our aggressiveness. They do not go toward educating us as to who we really are or what our racial group could actually accomplish in our homeland.

If wealthy slaves and compassionate whites were to donate money to assist in paying someone to think for our slave nation, and us alone, this would be money well spent. And, we would see results if the proper checks and balances were put into place. At least the benefactors would know for certain what they are getting for their money. Imagine what would happen if several wealthy slaves came together and chipped in on paying the cost for just one intelligent, forward thinking, unafraid descendant of slaves to think and work, not for himself, but for American Slaves alone. Our slave nation would have taken the first step toward becoming a free, prosperous nation.

If our elite were serious, any financially liberated slave could sell his Rolls Royce or multimillion dollar home and use the proceeds to pay someone to think our racial group through the first round of freedom. In fact, they should lead the charge to construct an advancement plan for their people, then they really would be "giving back." Each American Slave must do his or her part as we struggle on the economic battlefield.

When I realized our elite were not aware of our people and our condition, or of how to help us, I was left with little choice: I was compelled to write this book. I had to let them know that there are those of us who do understand how to move our nation forward. However, we can't do it without the help of our noted brothers and sisters and those slaves who are already in leadership positions. Those who 'got lucky' have the resources. We common slaves don't have the means to provide significant help. Ordinary slaves are not newsworthy; we are not in the public eye. I was talking to a high ranking African American politician who let me know in no uncertain terms that, according to statistics, no one cares or wants to hear what a lowly 'nigger' thinks about a bunch of other 'niggers.' This was when I first learned that the topic of slavery was a 'political hot potato,' according to some African Americans.

I harbor no ill feelings toward those slaves who are well-connected, wealthy, famous, or educated. In fact, I am proud of their accomplishments. Still, it is my inherited duty to tell them that, because of who they are and the duties left them by our ancestors, they were and still are being misled by our discriminatory system. They have been tricked with doubletalk, hoodwinked by success, lead astray because of ignorance, and then cut out of the herd by the masters. ❖

CHAPTER 31

Giving Back is Painless
(Not caring is crippling)

When the descendants of slaves were marching in Birmingham, the local ministers, with the exception of Dr. King's lieutenants, were kept ignorant of Dr. King's strategies. This intelligence vacuum allowed the Birmingham officials to pit the local Negro ministers against Dr. King. They used the same slander and doubletalk used to divide our foreparents during slavery. They didn't even have to be creative in their technique because all descendants of slaves are inherently division-tainted toward each other, though few realize it.

White officials in Birmingham lied to the local Negro ministers and hoped they would never find out the truth of what Dr. King was really doing in their hometown. The ministers believed the negative rumors that were spread. But during Dr.

"The fact that America was built on the strength of slavery is seldom acknowledged. But, this is too important to the advancement of our culture to continue being disregarded."

King's incarceration, he prayed. His prayers inspired him to construct a stirring letter to the ministers outlining his motives and clarifying why he did what he did. Also, he explained why he didn't tell them his plans. He was in Birmingham because injustice was there, and he was compelled to carry the Gospel of "freedom" beyond his own hometown. It is the duty of our spiritual leaders, ministers, teachers and preachers to spread the word of freedom.

Those ministers, like today's, had forgotten who they were. Not realizing their identity, they were unaware of this duty, and that all slaves are still in slavery together no matter their residence — even those of us who appear to have broken the shackles, changed our identity, moved to the suburbs and think we are already free.

When he wrote the letter, Reverend King's overall mission was nowhere near completion, but once truthful communication was established between him and the local ministers and they understood he was fighting for their freedom, too, even those religious leaders who didn't fully understand or were afraid to help at least wished Dr. King well.

Now, this is important for those of us who aren't wealthy, but would still like to give back to our people: When slaves speak knowledgeably of our heritage, and the words are not merely lip service, or when slaves truly wish other slaves well no matter their status or the situation, they are automatically "giving back to our people." Acknowledging who we are is a change in our individual disposition that rises above and beyond our inherent, slave-hater mindset. It neutralizes our inborn shame.

When the alienated ministers truly wished Dr. King well, they caused the scales of justice to automatically tip in favor of integration because this united them mentally, and it alienated the insidious whites who were acting as if they wanted to unite with the Negro ministers, but were instead using the ministers' lack of knowledge to turn them against Dr. King.

Dr. King showed these ministers how to give back without it costing them anything, except taking just a few moments to candidly look at the events taking place around them, and then consider who they really were in regard to the events — *this could happen to us now.*

"If we follow the trail of slavery up to now, open our mind, and then learn how to see and comprehend the picture that we are looking at, we will start to understand the necessity of slavery to the American plan. We will begin to understand who we are. We're the people in the plan — we're the descendants of those slaves."

If we look carefully at the world around us we see that America is a primary leader in global industry, but America wouldn't have become successful without certain events taking place as planned. If we visualize America from her existence, we can't help but see the role slavery played in these proceedings. If we follow the trail of slavery up to now, open our mind, and then learn how to see and comprehend the picture that we are looking at, we will start to understand the necessity of slavery to the American plan. We will begin to understand who we are. We're the people in the plan — *we're the descendants of those slaves.*

Once we know who we are, and then realize what America has become, it's not too difficult to surmise how and why our people were bred to be slaves — *slaves were needed to help build America and serve white Americans.* Slaves were, still are, and always will be a permanent part of the very *foundation of America.*

Even today, slavery's aftereffects still dictate how business is done in America. The fact that America was built on the strength of slavery is seldom acknowledged but this is too important to the advancement of our true culture to continue being disregarded.

Descendants of slaves must be made aware: Other racial groups already comprehend who we are; they just don't talk about it in our presence. For slaves to acquire a positive attitude toward our ethnicity, we must be told our real identity, and then we must accept these facts. These truths are the only foundation on which we can build future development. This African American fantasy that our leaders conjured up is not just shaky ground — it is a damaging fallacy!

Now, this is important: All slaves don't have to be on the front lines in the heat of battle to give back to our people or for our group to break free of slavery and prosper. Individual slaves just recognizing and then admitting who they are (*even if it is only to themselves*) would release positive vibes into the atmosphere in relation to American Slaves. If our leaders were to appreciate who we are and let leaders from other ethnic groups see they are not ashamed of us and are proud to be leading us, we ordinary slaves would stop being embarrassed about our heritage. This positive charge would fuse itself into racial pride — *it would fill the air* — it would cause the scales of justice to tip in favor of freedom for all descendants of American Slaves.

Freedom in America is commercially based. Wealthy slaves

"When I realized that my funds were being used to help most everyone else, instead of my own people, I made myself a promise: I will help American Slaves — exclusively — until we are truly freed, or until my demise."

are financially free, individually, but the bulk of our people are still in bondage, both mentally and economically.

Just like America needed slaves back then, our people need this book now. This book is an important informational tool that has been missing. It is written to let ordinary descendants of slaves know that they are not forgotten. There is a *way* for successful slaves to give back to our people and purchase our racial freedom at the same time, and it won't cost any more than many are currently contributing to other groups.

Be aware: The United Negro College Fund, the National Council of Negro Women, the National Political Congress of Black Women, the NAACP, the Urban League, the Rainbow Coalition, and there are others, all have their constituencies, (and they do serve real purposes), but none of them straightforwardly address the descendants of American Slaves' special, growing needs.

Now, are slaves still "colored people" to the NAACP, or have we turned 'black,' or have they conceded to the term African American? Regardless of where they stand at the moment, it is clear they do not solely target the descendants of American Slaves.

The reason black businesspersons, athletes, entertainers and other professional descendants of slaves who are wealthy, give large donations to predominantly white colleges, all black colleges, charities and churches, is because there is no program, charity, or church that these powerful people can give to that exclusively addresses the special needs of their people, the descendants of American Slaves. If there were such an organization, optimistically, these influential people would support it.

When I realized I had been filling the pockets of charities and helping the wrong people, it hurt me deeply because I had been blindly watching my own community of people suffer, but I didn't know what I was looking at. It was whites who taught me how to be a successful American minority. It was also whites who taught me how to decrease my tax liability by giving money to charity to help my community, but not one time did they tell me that I was a slave! When I became aware of my identity and realized that my funds were being used to help most everyone else, instead of my own people, I made myself a promise. I will help American Slaves — exclusively — until we are truly freed, or until my demise. Hopefully, I am not the only descendant of slaves who feels this way.

Slaves who have escaped poverty by breaking through the barriers are supposed to work together and figure out ways to come back and assist their people. At least this is what our ancestors used to do once they had successfully escaped. This is what Harry Belafonte was doing when he made funds available to help Dr. King and the movement out of a tight spot.

Harry Belafonte wasn't always on the front lines, in person, yet he went above and beyond the call of duty for his people. When Dr. King's followers were jailed and Dr. King couldn't get them out on bond, the famous entertainer, a well-known, esteemed descendant of slaves, dug deep into his own pockets and then persuaded others to dig deep, also. They came up with the much needed bail money. Mr. Belafonte successfully gave back to *his people*. And his giving didn't put him in the poorhouse, either. Above all, he knew exactly where his contribution went and what it achieved. The descendants of slaves never forget these unselfish heroes who are fighting to free our people. When Mr. Belafonte gave back to his people, he carved his name profoundly into American Slave history.

Powerful descendants of slaves are making a wonderful gesture contributing to charities, to special interest groups, and to communities, but these monies could better be invested to help free *our* people. Charity begins at home. ❖

> *"Slaves who have escaped poverty by breaking through the barriers are supposed to work together and figure out ways to come back and assist their people. At least this is what our ancestors used to do once they had successfully escaped."*

CHAPTER 32

I Ain't No House Nigger!

(I'm a big-time racial leader)

It is doubtful that any of our current leaders would admit to being Uncle Toms, but do they know what an Uncle Tom is? An Uncle Tom is a descendant of slaves who is in a leadership position. He sees his people's lesser condition and he knows they are being racially abused, but he doesn't 'feel it.' Another definition of an Uncle Tom is the good, upstanding slave descendant who has reached a higher status, accumulated wealth, and then is allowed limited access into the white world. He is usually thought of as a pillar in our society; however, there is a problem. Much too often, he has forgotten who he is and who his people are. At this point, he may not be a fully accredited Uncle Tom, but he is an Uncle Tom candidate. How do I know this — I was once a nominee.

This type of candidate sus-

> *"The worst and most damaging Uncle Tom of all is the Tom who doesn't have a clue that he is, or could ever be one. However, he is easily recognizable because he is usually a prosperous preacher or a rich business man, a vocal politician, or a high profile 'racial leader.'"*

pects his people are thinking he is an Uncle Tom, but he's not sure. He didn't set out to become one — it just happened. He was given a raise in pay, or in stature, and then, unknowingly, he was thrust into an Uncle Tom posture. Once he learns how to outthink and outmaneuver the uninformed people of his racial group and gets a taste of white freedom, he thinks to himself, "Hmm — not bad at all!" He is hooked. He begins to look down his nose at the lowest of his people the same as white racists have always done. This person qualifies as a snobbish Uncle Tom.

Since slavery, several types of Uncle Toms have surfaced. The worst and most damaging Uncle Tom of all is the Tom who doesn't have a clue that he is, or could ever be one. However, he is easily recognizable because he is usually a prosperous preacher or a rich business man, a vocal politician, or a high profile 'racial leader.' The reason he thinks he could never be a Tom is because he mistakenly assumes he is helping his people. Every time there is a racial problem, or any situation related to race, these publicity hounds scramble to get in front of the TV cameras with or without their bullhorns and spread their worthless rancor. Those of us who hail them as leaders should be aware; they are not leaders at all; they are noisy Uncle Toms doing their well-thought-out, well-rehearsed, leader impersonation.

Temptation is Uncle Tom bait

We must be clear on how some descendants of slaves wound up being Uncle Toms, yet are unaware of it. 'African American' leaders of today head nonprofit corporations and some programs that are government-sponsored or government-sanctioned. These organizations are endorsed by the United States because they are supposed to assist inner-city dwellers in upgrading their lives. The leaders of these organizations typically receive sizable salaries derived from contributions. This high remuneration is explained as necessary to remove the temptation of bribery, payoffs, collusion, kickbacks, conflicts of interest, and other forms of double dipping. It's not practical to get into a position to lead the people and then use your leadership position to compete against the people you are supposed to be leading. Slave leaders who do this are classified as blatant Uncle Toms. They just don't care, and that's putting it mildly.

> *"American Slaves will never get free if the leadership of our community continues competing against each other for crumbs, while plain workaday descendants of slaves are mentally enslaved."*

I reason that wealthy descendants of slaves have never sought to pay intellectuals to chart the way for our people because they see the ineffectiveness of those who head various nonprofit corporations and who are reportedly already engaged in leading and thinking for us. Instead of leading us, many get greedy, open a business, and then start competing against us. When they are not holding us back with this illegal, cutthroat tactic, they spend their time thinking of new ways to compete against each other in order to keep their individual pockets filled.

American Slaves will never get free if the leadership of our community continues competing against each other for crumbs, while plain workaday descendants of slaves are mentally enslaved. For our people to be free, we must stop the greed, combine our mentalities, and learn to work together as an organized force with a clear mission. ❖

CHAPTER 33

Mass Misconception

(A product bred from mass misunderstanding)

At one time, 'black' was the worst thing a slave could be called; however, things have changed. Presently, whenever I hear the word black, I think of commerce because blackness now has the power to boost TV ratings.

It's because unaware descendants of slaves view noted black

> "Our role models are misleading our people into coping with existing abuse and teaching us to expect future abuse."

entertainers as their role models that commercial blackness could be hurtful to slaves as a people. In most cases, these performers are getting paid big bucks to sell "blackness" at the expense of American Slaves.

Because of our state of mind, no one pays too much attention to black comedians making jokes about the American Slaves' ghetto lifestyle. Television has taught us to laugh at our condition today just as slaves were reduced to humor in order to cope during slavery. However, back then there was nothing our ancestors could do about their atrocious circumstance.

Our role models are misleading our people into coping with existing abuse and teaching us to expect future abuse. When Slave comics have talent, and their jokes sound funny enough, their yarns are accepted as being humorous. Therefore, our condition is not thought of as miserable, but instead as an accepted, amusing lifestyle. Victims finding humor in the way they and their loved ones are mistreated would seem to signify that their condition is acceptable.

There are ways for African American entertainers to offset this exploitation of our people, but only if they will accept their true identity. If they knew who they were, knew our mission and wanted to be a part of our team, they could actually help spread the word of freedom by publicly wishing their own nation well at the same time they are selling blackness at our expense.

If whites were being abused, I don't think they would find it funny at all. From what I have learned about whites, they wouldn't accept being laughed at for being second-class citizens who are perpetually mistreated. Whites would think about it, get their heads together, and then *collectively* they would do something about it.

More mass misconception

Racial jokes are one thing, but when descendants of slaves start *rapping* about the maltreatment they receive in America, this is a whole new ball game — something must be done, and quick! Our angry rappers have a large following, which is tempting to TV networks, also. However, these rappers aren't trying to boost ratings, nor are they trying to get laughs at our expense. Their message is hate, and some of it is directed at whites. Rapping about doing harm to "Mr. Charlie" is totally unacceptable.

Have anxious whites looked at the hostility expressed in rap music as rappers reaching out in pain, trying to show their discontent? Slave leaders are constantly complaining about the subjective lyrics of rap music. They say the message is hate, but have they thought in depth about some of the 'hateful' communication? This hate didn't just now start, and it didn't start during our integration struggle or the civil rights movement. When we realize who we are, we will understand that this hatred stems from the abuse that slaves have always received — *long before the Civil War.* It started during slavery and it hasn't slowed down. It just has different symptoms and takes on a different look according to what time period we are living in. During slavery, it was hangings and floggings. During our integration encounter, it was dogs and fire hoses. Now, it's disguised discrimination — *sometimes in the form of bullets!*

Pressure from the system, by way of some of our noted Uncle Toms, did make a few rappers tone their rap down in regards to threatening Mr. Charlie, but most just started rapping about lowdown smut and internal violence. They

"There are ways for African American entertainers to offset this exploitation of our people, but only if they will accept their true identity. If they knew who they were, knew our mission and wanted to be a part of our team, they could actually help spread the word of freedom by publicly wishing their own nation well at the same time that they are selling blackness at our expense."

pulled their pants down and started talking dirty towards our women — seemingly more acceptable to whites *and* Uncle Toms.

Shrewd leaders would try to understand why these youngsters are discontented. Caring leaders would consider what they are rapping about as a warning of things to come if things don't change. Well, things did change, but only for the few rappers who made it out of the 'hood. Nothing has changed for the many street corner rappers that whites never hear from who are still ghetto-bound.

If there is justification for slaves making jokes about our racial condition and rappers degrading our women, influencing our young, and leading them down the wrong path, perhaps it is that they may be relating to our people's condition in the only way they know how. Our racial group has no viable leadership. These gifted slaves have no positive, racial image to look up to, or proper dialogue to follow. They make up their channel of communication as they go along, from the way they feel. The elders of our group seem unaware that our youngest and most vulnerable are following these rappers. This should tell us something about where our people are headed. It should also show America what could be lurking up ahead.

I must admit I do understand how our youngsters feel because, before I discovered my identity, I felt beaten down by the system, too. I related to life in an entirely different manner. My attitude probably appeared unenthusiastic to whites within our political system. Some of my elders chided me for being a hell-raiser and having a negative attitude. Looking back, I realize I didn't have a negative attitude.

When looking closely at slavery, we see that during slavery our population was programmed to be 'gentle.' Overall, slaves have always had gentle, lighthearted attitudes. However, when we look closer, we see that a depressed state of mind was brutally instilled into our foreparents. The aftereffect is evident in present-day descendants of slaves and is often mistaken for unconstructive attitudes.

As we listen to our rappers and what they are saying, we must keep in mind the lack of hope affects people differently. Similarly situated people often show their frustrations in different ways. The elders in my old neighborhood might have known my frustrations, but they didn't know how to help me. They had no idea how to help a slave. Our leaders of today don't either because the leadership of our group has yet to realize we are slaves.

My elders told me many times that I should try to better myself, but they didn't give me any direction. Like youngsters of today, I wasn't about to listen to "them ol' darkies." To my way of thinking at that time I was faring better than a lot of them. Consequently, why should I do what they say? I was like young slaves are today — hardheaded. I thought I already knew everything.

It wasn't until I became fully aware I was descended from slaves that I could decipher the elders' words. Their heartfelt message flowed back into my soul and started eating away at the thick layer of my inherited ignorance. As my head eased and my emotions subsided, I could see that, even though the elders were naïve, they were truly trying to help me. Looking back, I can see how I was actually hurting my people.

I have since changed my life. I now express myself the way I feel descendants of slaves at this juncture in our journey are supposed to express themselves — truthfully. At this point, our greatest needs are for accurate information and easy-to-follow direction.

Exposure

There is a possibility that African American leaders might not recognize these truths right away and, if they were to identify with these facts, they might be apprehensive about going public. They might prefer being 'closet slaves.' This, I understand. A significant undertaking will be to teach our current leaders how to follow orders unerringly and faithfully whether they are 'closet slaves' or not.

Some of these leaders are apprehensive to the point that they have said my point of view is bizarre. They make it clear they think I'm a little strange. Well, to me, the truth of who I am is not bizarre — *it's fact*.

Facts are what caused me to no longer be ashamed of whom I am. Now, I really do like who I am. I don't think it should be considered out of the ordinary 'for me to be me.' Being myself, I can get the true message out, *and that feels good!* Why would anyone think it's strange for a human being to want to embrace who he is? It's the only way one can work toward improvement. It seems peculiar to me that, in an intelligent setting, our leaders would try to pass us off as someone other than who we are. The bizarreness of the American Slave situation is that these people who have the nerve to call themselves our leaders haven't figured some of these things out. It's their job. It's what our ancestors left for them to do.

There is no excuse for the current, sorry state of slave leadership. We have had more than a century to get our act together. The facts of slavery are right before our faces; yet, our leaders still can't decipher who we are.

Because of white brutality, many slaves are leery of offending whites with this new consciousness. Because whites are in charge in this country and still in control of our racial group, some descendants of slaves actually think white leaders already fully grasp the overall condition of the descendant of slaves but lack the interest to do anything about it. This is a terrible misconception. Every white that I have talked with would love to help us (well, *almost* every white). However, as it stands, as long as our leaders will not acknowledge who we are — no one can help us!

Meaningless articulation

African American leaders try to be 'political' when they talk to whites. Our two cultures don't indulge in straight talk about racial issues. Descendants of slaves and descendants of slave masters may labor under the same roof at places of employment. We might communicate openly about current events that are wide-ranging and generic and sometimes even hang out together, socially, even to the point of marriage and having children, but we are still *not on speaking terms to each other when it relates to the subject of slavery.* 'African American' leaders don't know how to start a collective slavery dialogue that includes all descendants of slaves. Not understanding slavery keeps our two people from understanding each other.

> *"There is no excuse for the current, sorry state of slave leadership. We have had more than a century to get our act together. The facts of slavery are right before our faces; yet, our leaders still can't decipher who we are."*

I talked openly with whites about the importance of slavery to America, and how I felt about slavery, and those whites, themselves. I didn't want there to be any misconception. I wanted to know their difficulty in accepting this concept of slavery. They informed me that this new message is not offensive at all. In fact, most whites asked what they could do to help. Some wanted to know what they could do to keep from hurting the descendants of slaves further. Once whites heard the underlying aftereffects of slavery, some came to understand they had been prejudiced all along, but didn't even realize it.

Whites are an intelligent people when it comes to the welfare of our country. I sincerely believe if intelligent communication (coupled with the facts) was injected into the American Slaves' situation, whites would understand why we are hurting, largely in silence. I deeply believe that once whites hear from a slave, how slaves *actually* feel, they will empathize.

Overall, whites are not opposed to the fair treatment of American Slaves, but whites won't help slaves if slaves don't ask for help. And that's a problem. In our minds, a slave is the last thing we would ever want to be. Our leaders — thinking they are merely 'African Americans' — would never ask for help for slave descendants.

In my own neighborhood, there are many who are irritated at me because I say we are descended from slaves; that we are and always will be slaves until we are freed legally. Some of my neighbors have spouted verbal abuse at me; others have quit speaking to me altogether. They don't understand that I am trying to help all descendants of slaves.

Toward the latter part of 2003, the electrical contractors were hanging out our nation's 'first shingle,' a beautiful, brightly lit sign that declared our racial identity. I wanted the world to know that American Slaves are alive and well, and ready to do business. I was proud because I had lettered the sign myself. A perturbed mother accompanied by two youngsters approached me. I greeted her with my proudest and brightest smile, but she didn't smile back. Instead, she vented her rage. She exclaimed, "Mr. Shelton, you should be ashamed of yourself, confusing our children and putting all of that nonsense and foolishness in these young people's head. Don't we have enough problems without you stirring up trouble?"

When I tried to explain, she stomped off in a huff.

Even though I have survived a very turbulent life, which has included many ups and downs, this mother caused me to question myself and the continued existence of our people. Her words cut deep, bringing back the sickening pain of slavery. On this night I despaired, not for myself, but for my people.

Once our people are accurately identified and properly structured, our leaders who are at the top of our group must begin immediately teaching us the truth. The truth will direct how we relate to each other. Then we will have a better understanding of how to relate to whites.

I'm still just an ignorant slave — help me understand!

Mr. Randall Robinson wrote a book, *The Debt: What America Owes to Blacks.* His book partially addresses compensation for 'blacks.' This is the same kind of doubletalk that adds to slave ignorance and makes it almost impossible to help the descendants of slaves.

The debt that is owed for slavery perpetrated in America is owed to American Slaves and their descendants only, not all blacks. If slaves are to be paid the debt owed to American Slaves, we had better get the facts straight first. These specifics must be in writing and able to stand up under close scrutiny.

Slaves did the work, they took the abuse, and they were instrumental in the building of America. Their descendants are the only ones who should be compensated for slavery in America.

Those educated slaves who are in leadership positions must know to be cautious in how they use words in relation to the descendants of American Slaves. During slavery, brutal violence intimidated our ancestors, but bad information has enslaved our people's overall mentality, perpetually. I could understand an ordinary, ghetto descendant of slaves making so terrible an error out in public, but I hear this Robinson fellow is supposed to be smart. It appears he doesn't fully comprehend the nature of the debt! Maybe he's not descended from American Slaves.

The cruelty of floggings and other brutal violence kept the field hands in chains and on their knees, but devious language was one of the tools used by the master to keep the 'house niggers' enslaved. They, in turn, helped keep the slaves beneath them in virtual shackles, using the same words the master taught them. Nothing has changed!

Highly-schooled descendants of slaves, who lack common sense, are nothing more than well-trained parrots. They are prime candidates to become ignorant leaders. After they accomplish this feat, they pass on their ignorance to their followers.

American Slaves are already uninformed, and these educated guys don't have the decency to coach us with common sense intelligence. These types of leaders don't know it, but they reinforce their followers' ignorance by writing without thinking and continually saying the wrong thing in public. If it is a big word, they'll use it, but won't even take the time to explain what the word means to their ignorant followers and what affect it might have upon them. Inherent ignorance and a lack of common sense causes this type of leader to misunderstand what others are saying — and they're too ashamed to ask what is being said. They don't realize the damage their erroneous terminology, misdirection, and misunderstanding of expressions does to our people.

Mr. Robinson was also one of two 'African Americans' who shared a split television screen on a telecast one day. They were expounding on reparations for slavery for *African Americans*.

These TV guests didn't seem to know it but, with all of their education, prestige, and false reputation, they were using the same type of doubletalk the slave masters used to influence our ancestors' mentality. The entire TV debate was doubletalk because neither guest called us who we are.

I strongly suspect they were really talking about the descendants of American Slaves when they were using the words black, and African American. If that was the case, they were on the right track; they just didn't say it correctly.

Mr. Keys suggested that, because of Ms. Oprah Winfrey's status and wealth, Mr. Robinson would have a hard time persuading her she was due reparations. He thinks the way some slaves and many ignorant racists think: If one or two slave descendants, or whatever we are called at the moment, have a little money, people perceive our entire population as doing well. Of course, that's not true.

> *"Highly schooled descendants of slaves who don't have common sense are nothing more than well-trained parrots. They are prime candidates to become ignorant leaders. After they accomplish this feat, they pass on their ignorance to their followers."*

It is my sincere opinion that these gentlemen truly wish to help their people but they are part of the problem. They are out in front of the masses passing themselves off as our leaders, and passing their ignorance on to us as well . It seems obvious these fellows don't even know who they are.

If the descendants of slaves are not like-minded on getting our section of the American population together before receiving any reparations, racial confusion will spread like a virus; things could get out of hand. Once our politicians fully understand we are descendants of slaves and not African Americans, they should understand our *real* problem.

American Slaves must not be afraid of hurting inadequate leaders' feelings no matter how famous they are, how powerful they think they are, or how dangerous they try to make us think they are. We must face this leadership void head-on, trusting that right will win in the long run. ❖

CHAPTER 34

Influence in the 'Hood

(The initial attack)

I must admit writing a frank treatise about my racial identity and what I have seen and believe concerning our inner cities is not something I looked forward to. But I understood the significance of such a delicate mission and the many stumbling blocks any writer, black or white, would surely encounter dealing with this type of shameful, degrading subject matter.

"There are many descendants of slaves who have written about slavery, and also our inner cities, but they have yet to make a positive, racial impression on people of our slave nation."

The reason why slavery hasn't been properly documented before is because documentation is evidence. The reason slavery hasn't been dealt with before is because human beings have a tendency to deal with things and events that are pleasing to the individual. It's a natural instinct. That is why the cover-up of slavery has gone on this long. Whites would rather not deal with the ugliness of slavery, or the cost to rectify it. And slave descendants have grown accustomed to slavery.

There are many descendants of slaves who have written about slavery, and also our inner cities, but they have yet to make a positive, racial impression for people of our slave nation.

Ordinary slaves don't have the capability to reason that slavery was an atrocious act intended to silently perpetuate itself using weak, ignorant leadership as the main vehicle. Willie Lynch brought this to public attention 300 years ago. Slaves of old might not have been able to read his letter at that time, but since then we have learned how to read. It seems that some among us should have figured out our perpetual ignorance and how it is perpetuated by now.

Scrutinizing the 'hood

Normally, when we look at inner-city neighborhoods the first thing we see is that, from the time when Dr. King was assassinated, we have lost control of them. The second thing we see is that we have lost a large number of our children to evil elements, and that isn't all.

When we look at inner-cities as a whole, we see that some of our children might have strayed. However realistically, we have never consciously had control of our neighborhoods. Our racial group was born in slavery, baptized in ignorance, and then released into poverty, where we have been forced to remain. Foreigners and immigrants largely control our neighborhoods because they usually operate the 'mom and pop' stores that control our neighborhood economy. There was a time when we had control of our children, but the present generation is quickly slipping away. I believe we could bring our children back if we had something tangible to offer them, or if they had something positive to come back to.

To see our inner-city problems clearly we must fine-tune our mental vision. Once properly adjusted, we see that the most noticeable symptom of the aftereffects of slavery in our inner-

"Foreigners and immigrants largely control our neighborhoods, because they usually operate the 'mom and pop' stores that control our neighborhood economy."

city neighborhoods is not the loss of our youth, but their losing respect for their elders. When I was a youngster, children were taught to respect their elders. There was a special sentiment that bonded our group. Home training was an expression among our people that had a far-reaching effect.

It was common practice for neighborhood elders to help the many single-parent families in our inner cities with their child-care and young adult disciplining. They didn't baby-sit, but if a neighborhood youth was acting up, any neighborhood elder could set him straight. That wasn't the end of it. When he got home, home training was poised and waiting. Young descendants of slaves were obedient and strong-minded compared to today's disrespectful, undisciplined, and sometimes hostile, young slave descendants who are unconsciously taught to be ashamed of slavery.

When we look closer, we see that slave parents of today aren't allowed to rear their children properly according to whom we are. Presently, slave parents must stay within guidelines that were set up to guide free whites, or other nationalities that have had hundreds, even thousands, of years of home training. Because of these guidelines, the bulk of our young are denied the guidance a young, undeveloped nation needs. This can only come from *strict*, in-home discipline; proper identity; and the *initial* installation of pride.

A juvenile nation must be given reasons to hope for the future. Then each individual in the nation must come to understand racial discipline and why it's required because of their heritage. If we want our group to be equal to whites in the future, we need to give our children the special training they need today. This special home training must become a permanent part of our racial plan.

If descendants of slaves can't retake and then control our own neighborhoods and our own children in the name of American Slaves, how will we ever be able to secure our freedom and then control our racial destiny?

Dissecting the shame of slavery

After the Civil War, whites tricked the slaves into thinking they were liberated Negroes. In ignorance, the slaves scattered, drifting aimlessly without direction and unaware of their true selves.

After the assassination of Dr. King, what little leadership that was left standing sputtered and the descendants of slaves drifted farther apart, causing us to wind up without internal leadership. An entire population of people without adequate leadership and internal control is a haven for individual clashes that could lead to racial unrest and possible disaster.

It must be because of the shame connected to slavery and,

therefore, to the descendants of slaves that our leaders started impersonating African Americans. I can't think of another reason why they would refuse to make slavery (the only thing for which America owes us) a fundamental, permanent part of our heritage. This imagined African American identity has caused slaves to have a negative attitude toward our true identity and our history. This negative approach is improperly influencing our young. Young slaves of today are even more opposed to facing slavery as African Americans than we were when we thought we were Negroes. Dr. King often talked of slavery, and of us being slaves. Since his assassination, our leaders are either scared or too ashamed to even use the word slave. Today, our people have respect for Africans, but we are disrespectful toward the elder descendants of slaves because they are still enmeshed in the old ways of obedience.

In America, discrimination is talked about constantly, but rarely in conjunction to slavery. Have you ever wondered why? America doesn't want descendants of slaves to know we are still slaves. Racial incidents are not directed at Africa or Africans — nor are they aimed at true African Americans. Racial bias in America is directed at those of us who are descended from slaves!

In my efforts to explore our racial shame, I discussed the descendants of slaves' identity crisis with young and old. Older descendants of slaves become angry when asked what racial group they belong, but none of them relate their negative behavior to slavery. When young slaves are asked what racial entity they belong to, they look confused, then hurt, as if asked a question they should know the answer to but don't. Meek and uncertain, they usually answer "African American," yet they seldom understand their meekness or wonder why they are uncertain. Neither young nor old could give me any logical reason why they thought they were African Americans.

With Dr. King gone, our young are left without adequate

racial leadership. The flashy, brash ways and financial trappings of pimps, whores, drug dealers, and other street people caught our children's eyes, and it didn't take long for the glitter of street life to lure them away from family influence and the watchful eyes of the neighborhood elders. This leadership vacuum made it relatively easy for delinquents, who learned all too quickly how to mimic street people, to apply peer pressure to our youth.

At a very young age, accumulated oppression causes descendants of slaves to feel their life is hopeless. Some of our elders should have realized by now that this hopelessness is a carryover from slavery. There is no way the children of our group can understand their oppression because the elders of our ethnic community never tell them about the cause — slavery.

Descendants of slaves live with undiagnosed subjugation all of their lives, and then they pass this defeatism on to future generations. When these same young slaves become elders, and have gained hindsight, it then becomes clear. They could have done better in life if they had only listened to their elders, but they are the elders now. Their life is almost over, and they still haven't realized who they are. They haven't accumulated any wealth; therefore, they haven't advanced any further in life than their ancestors. Truth be known, they have regressed because the rest of the world sped up, leaving them even further behind. It's clear to see that our nation is caught up in a 'going nowhere' circle.

Neighborhood exploitation

Missed opportunities by senior slaves and flashy trappings by 'player' slave descendants who influence our young, dictate that young people, not elders, influence inner-city neighborhoods today. Flashy descendants of slaves are parading, while older people have resorted to hiding behind closed doors. They are afraid or either ashamed to come into

"Flashy descendants of slaves are parading, while older people have resorted to hiding behind closed doors. They are afraid or ashamed to come into the streets and mingle with, or direct and correct, their own children."

the streets and mingle with, or direct and correct, their own children.

Potentially decent children take their cue from those neighborhood toughs who curse the loudest and behave the most outrageously. It's a submission thing. Children see fear displayed by neighborhood elders, so they capitulate to the villains that senior citizens are afraid of, and then they acquiesce to negative peer pressure. Young descendants of slaves are easily dazzled by fast, flashy, instant gratification. Can you blame them? The elders have nothing to offer these youngsters because they themselves are hurting.

Destitute children see no reason to wait for success, to labor in the trenches and wind up like their elders. They see many slaves who seem to "make it big" almost overnight through drug dealing, whoring, pimping and thievery.

The young slave may revere the stooped, old people who are living in poverty, even as they preach the virtue of earning your own way by the sweat of your brow, but it's hard for these youngsters to ignore the jewelry-laden pimp driving his Cadillac in the fast lane. Reverend Brown may look quite distinguished and may even have the inside track to heaven, but Bad Bad Leroy Brown seems to be having lots of fun right here on earth.

Following the rules didn't advance the elders because they were discriminated against and ignored. Being shut out they have lived their entire lives in poverty, ignorant of who they are and unaware of their birthright.

Sometimes our young are misled into thinking that breaking the rules and going against the law is beneficial, at least this is their perception. Therefore, this is the avenue some of them view as the road to successful living in our inner cities.

To make a bad situation worse, the neighborhood villains' respect for their elders was replaced with a combination of hate, mixed with fear, for the local police. The villains' handed-down-from-slavery ignorance cautions them to hate the white police, but their ingrained fear of whites compels them to fear these same police because they know some of these officers are taught early on not to take 'nigger prisoners.' The young lawbreaker gets further confused when he gets much the same treatment from the black officers as he gets from white law enforcement. This causes some of our young to not have respect for black police officers, most of whom are trying to be superior policemen and do a conscientious job.

The belligerent slave descendant believes the black police officer should give him a break because 'a brother' should understand what he is going through, but he reasons that the black police officer is an Uncle Tom who takes his orders from a 'nigger-hating' white boss. It will never cross his mind that, just maybe, this cop's boss is also black.

The police are perplexed because they don't understand why some descendants of slaves protect undesirables in their families. They get even more confounded when we protect thugs and lowlifes we don't even know. These officers overlook the fact that some of their fellow officers treat descendants of slaves as if we are animals, the same as evil whites treated our foreparents during slavery. The average slave knows, whether innocent or guilty, he will be automatically considered culpable by the average white police officer. Innocent slaves receiving the same mistreatment as guilty slaves causes an unconscious, unspoken bond to be created between all slaves.

Undeserved racial abuse and open discrimination results in slaves feeling empathy for other slaves (even the guilty); this is an aftereffect of slavery. Our underlying slave mentality knows that all descendants of slaves share the same heritage. In the back of our minds, we know that no matter what we call ourselves or where we reside, guilty or innocent, the majority of us will suffer white abuse at some time.

Sometimes when dealing with our ethnic group, insignificant incidents can get out of hand because no one involved realizes that not understanding slavery and its ignorant aftereffects are the real culprits behind racially motivated, inner-city flare-ups — not the descendants of slaves.

Elders don't chastise anymore because they don't understand our young or their need for flashy trappings; therefore, they are afraid of them. Often they are afraid of the police, too, because of the brutal violence some rogue cops demonstrate when dealing with dark-skinned, inner-city dwellers. Fear of imminent violence, mixed with misunderstanding, curtails what elder slaves should be doing and what they could do best, which is help our people advance by molding our youth.

The younger generations of slaves view their elders as "old-fogies" because the seniors are telling their young what they should do to prosper. However, their advice falls on deaf ears because the picture the seniors are painting for their young doesn't resemble anything related to either's surroundings.

Senior slaves advise young slaves: If you want to get ahead in life, go to school, get an education, respect your parents, and do unto others as you would have others do unto you. All of this advice is sound. However, the slave children notice the deplorable conditions surrounding the older person who has always tried to live by these rules. They conclude that "trying to do right" just got their elders more degradation. They question what seniors base their advice on, and then wonder: Why didn't you 'old niggers' try your own advice if it works so well?

I have actually heard young descendants of slaves respond to their elders in this hopeless manner when elders try to advise them. This creates a continuing ghetto cycle. Because, when young slaves disregard sound elder advice, they are left with a much lesser option — to draw from each other's misery instead of their elders' experience. Most young descendants of slaves want to do well in life, but the majority of our young have scant hope.

Younger inner-city slaves can't comprehend what the elders "are yapping about" and since many of our youth are faring better than their elders, they have nothing to relate any higher hope to, except television, which has been known to glorify violence and crime in inner-city neighborhoods but seldom provides hope for the descendants of American Slaves.

Commonsense thinking

Inner-city unrest and racial disturbances that turn into riots are usually the result of leaders not knowing, not caring, or not admitting who the darker-skinned, inner-city dwellers are. Disorders are usually quelled with quick fixes that postpone the next uprising. The repair never gets to the core because slavery is never discussed. If inner-city unrest is to cease, and if inner

Old people, living in poverty, preach the virtue of earning your own way by the sweat of your brow, but it's hard for youngsters to ignore the jewelry-laden pimp driving his Cadillac in the fast lane.

cities are to change for the better, understanding slaves and slavery's aftereffects must be taken into consideration.

To finally and fully abolish slavery, we must provide inner-city dwellers with a better understanding of slavery and an adequate program that will establish them in mainstream America. This program must not be confused with neighborhood or minority programs. There is a big difference between these programs and a countrywide, *slave nation*, program.

Inner-city unrest, in most cases, is a direct result of racial abuse, which is caused by the hate that ignorance breeds. Poverty is the undeniable result of this racially abusive ignorance.

White leaders confirm their own ignorance by allowing racial abuse to continue in an environment they control. Slave leaders confirm our people's ignorance by not recognizing our racial ignorance and fear of confronting white leaders about slavery. ❖

CHAPTER 35

Where Do We Go From Here?

(The ultimate goal of every slave — freedom!)

To arrive at this juncture in my life, my first step was to acknowledge my true identity; then I had to openly and verbally admit to other slaves, and to whites, that I am a descendant of slaves — not African American! The second step is proving to be more difficult because, not only do I have

> *"My ultimate goal is to be truly free, but I can't reach my goal until I live up to my inherited obligation, which is to help as much as one person can to finish freeing our people."*

to accept the fact that I am *still* a slave in order to reach my goal (which is to help my people), I must persuade others they are still slaves, too. That's going to take some serious doing. That's why I had to 'go back home' — *all the way to slavery.*

At first, revisiting slavery was depressing, upsetting and mind-boggling. But then when it seemed as if I would find no answers to my peoples' problem, my prayers were answered, my mind was cleansed, and hundreds of years of being infected with racial ignorance was washed away. Today, I am a new man; my mind is refreshed and my spirit is high. I openly brag that I am an American Slave — *and it feels great!*

My ultimate goal is to be truly free. However I can't reach that goal until I live up to my inherited obligation, which is to help as much as one person can to finish freeing our people. I cannot be truly free, not even in death, if my group is still mentally enslaved and I didn't do all I could to help them break free.

Boom, burst, or busted

Racial leaders and politicians, who sit in with the city fathers when they have their strategy meetings to decide the direction of their respected cities, think they are utterly free, but they are not. They are bound by an ongoing responsibility to their people, by way of their ancestors, they are unable to break free from because it's a moral obligation that hasn't been fulfilled. Some of these wanna-be leaders could fulfill their inherited, ethnic obligation. They could help free their people and it wouldn't cost them anything. They only need to share vital information that could help advance our nation.

Slave leaders have access to key information, connections, power, and influence that is vital to our racial growth, but ignorance keeps them from sharing the knowledge that helped them break free and permitted them to prosper. They must learn that it's not only OK, but necessary that they provide helpful information to other slave descendants who are in business and who are willing to help our people. If we had learned this simple tactic during our civil rights struggle, our 'buy black' campaign would have had a better chance at success.

The average slave descendants who are trying their hand at business are not affiliated with the system, and they have no way to get connected. This causes them to be routinely omitted from the decision-making process. We are also excluded from being

"The police don't understand why some descendants of slaves protect undesirables in their families. ... The average slave knows, whether innocent or guilty, he will be automatically considered culpable by the average white police officer."

general contractors, general managers, and other 'high-up generals' — unless we are politically connected. Meaningful opportunities and large indentures are almost exclusively issued to major corporations that are usually owned by whites or foreigners. Much of the time, if a descendant of slaves is in a high-up position in one of these companies he is merely a front for the company — an Uncle Tom.

Politicians and managers in charge of issuing contracts of any size use the excuse that our people can't handle jobs of such a large magnitude. This is another way our racial group is kept out of the mainstream U.S. economy. Much of the time these power-brokers are right, but there are legitimate reasons why descendants of slaves can't compete or perform at the highest levels. The most obvious reason is that we are openly discriminated against.

It's next to impossible for American Slaves to move up in American life because we never get the exposure or the hands-on experience, that is so essential to compete in the marketplace at the highest level. Theory alone is not adequate. Standing on the sideline, watching the white population grow even wealthier, doesn't help either.

If those descendants of slaves whom we consider our leaders, were our leaders, and if they were serious about giving back to their people, or *knew how to give back* to their people, they could help eliminate the discrimination that keeps us divided and, thereby, commercially handicapped.

For instance, a building boom is happening across America. In many areas, the slave quarters (which are now called ghettos, tenements, housing projects, or inner-city neighborhoods) are being rehabilitated. Some of these structures are buildings that were burned out in protest after Dr. King was treacherously assassinated. Older structures are coming down, and new structures are going up everywhere, and if older structures happen to survive this massive rebuilding, they are deemed historical monuments and then brought up to code. This is creating many jobs.

'African American' leaders see this rebuilding as a positive (and it is), but they can't see the whole picture. They see the neighborhood's condition, but they can't see their people's condition. They don't realize what they are witnessing is neighborhood restoration that is customary for the time period we are living in and should be done by the local dwellers. They suppose 'African Americans' are advancing because of the amount of money being spent on the slave descendants' neighborhoods. But money is not being spent *in* our neighborhoods. Money is being *made* in our neighborhoods, at our expense, because whites, Uncle Toms, and foreigners are the ones who are making the money — not us!

If a closer look is taken at our neighborhood renaissance, we realize slaves don't own the real estate and they don't own the businesses on the real estate. In some cases, the government practically gave whites and foreigners the property, initially, because they were game enough to invest their money in low value properties that are inhabited by slaves.

Descendants of slaves rarely get a chance to win bids on profitable jobs. When we are lucky enough to get in on one of these jobs we don't make much money, and then aren't allowed to handle the money. In short, descendants of slaves *still* do slave labor, take orders, and get abused.

Since the time American Slaves were freed (abandoned), our government has never encouraged us nor helped us as a people. Since the riots, no one has told us that we could, and should, own the profitable businesses being built and operated in our backyards. Due to lack of communication, the average of our people don't understand why we can't afford the houses that are being redeveloped in our own neighborhoods, unless there is some kind of subsidy.

It is disheartening to slave contractors when they see whites and foreigners gobble up property (at a low price) located in slave neighborhoods, get discounted loans to build with, and then charge slaves rent they can't afford. In most cases, black contractors can't buy prime properties because they are often earmarked for whites, foreigners, or good 'ol boys who are connected to the system. But, even if these properties weren't earmarked, in most cases, slaves lack adequate, financial backing to purchase them.

It's frightening that some slave politicians are overseeing parts of this massive rebuilding. They couldn't really understand what they are looking at — *they just think they do*. The spotlight of prestige has blinded them, but they are unaware of it!

The ghettos are being refurbished, but the descendants of American Slaves are not being elevated. We are omitted from the moneymaking end of it and the intelligence gathering that can be derived from this type of redevelopment; yet, this type of improvement is at the heart of the American dream. Descendants of slaves are never given the opportunity to redevelop their own neighborhoods because our leaders are tricked into introducing, and then being persuaded to vote in favor of passing, legislation which allows other racial groups (already knowledgeable of how to build and coordinate) to make money upgrading our stomping ground! If those who claim they are leading us knew our true identity, and understood the power that some of them could wield; they would organize us into a functioning group. Then they could introduce legislation that includes our own people. They could use their political power to create racial wealth and restore the vitality of our own neighborhoods, using our collective population as leverage. We could do what other racial groups are doing right under our noses — in *our* 'hoods.

If these politicians were astute, the minute they hear of any legislation coming up for vote that could be beneficial to their people, whether it is revitalizing neighborhoods or whatever, they would start constructing a plan to ensure slaves get the bulk of the benefits, or most of the money from these projects. That's what whites do. Of course, being a businessman and understanding how fast money goes, I would also insist that such contracts include a clause stating the descendants of slaves be given a chance to learn how to do everything that is being done at all levels.

Mangling the parable of the fisherman: Don't give one slave a fish sandwich because *he* is hungry; *that's individual charity.* Teach all American Slaves how to fish then we can feed our nation. As a people, we need know-how a lot more than we need insignificant assistance. Keep in mind, it was the lack of knowledge that enslaved our foreparents and left us shackled in our present, unaware condition.

Since I gained knowledge of self, my way of thinking has changed in regard to slavery and the future of American Slaves.

At first, being uninformed, like our current leaders, I wanted our reparations to be money. However, money for individuals is now a distant second to knowledge for our nation.

When the ghettos are finished being redeveloped and all of the money has been made, will American Slaves remain exactly where we have always been — submerged in ignorance? Will our neighborhoods be looking good while we are still relegated to the bottom? Will we be looking at what happened, but still wondering what happened? If we don't wake up, we will be the pawns of the game, and we still won't know the game is being played *on us*!

It is obvious our legislators don't know how to use our physical concentration in the ghettos and housing projects, and the inner city 'hoods, to our slave nation's advantage. They 'strut their stuff' while charting the way for the overall American populace, instead of focusing on *our* people. They take pride in voting on bills put before them, but they seldom create and introduce bills that will benefit their own people. African American leaders wouldn't have the ability to think up new ideas that would help American Slaves. They have made known they think 'niggers' are a lost cause. Many spend their time working on ideas that whites thought up. Our leaders are famous for solving white folks' problems, but they don't have a clue how to solve ours.

Redistricting bills and other pieces of legislation are being introduced that could block American Slaves' advancement. These bills dilute our presence by allowing whites, and 'wannabe whites' who have moved to the suburbs trying to get away from us, to cast votes on legislation that controls us. Some African American leaders are leading the charge to solicit our support and backing to bring this legislation to fruition. This legislation is nothing more than basic, long-range laws that usually hamper our racial progress. Our leaders don't know how to make these fundamental, but crucial maneuvers. This is another indication that our populace accepts being second-class citizens. We continually vote for, and follow, their pathetic leadership. ❖

CHAPTER 36

Racial Contribution
(Genetically induced labor)

*A*merican Slaves made the ultimate contribution to America, but since slavery the descendants of slaves are ignored until we take about as much abuse as we can stand. We then try to protest, but our protesting is always in vain because we are easily browbeaten back into 'our place.' At first, I couldn't put my finger on why we are deliberately ignored, then I realized: During slavery, slaves were forced to 'contribute' their labor to America. Is that what is expected of us still?

> "Those descendants of slaves who have the ability to contribute to America could help their people, if they weren't ashamed of whom we are."

Well, not always. Descendants of slaves who are politicians, sports figures, movie or TV stars, and so on, are high profile individuals. They are paid well because they do contribute to America. They have personal talents, skills, outstanding physical attributes, or an adequate education. Because of their attributes, these particular individuals are allowed access to the American mainstream and are often glorified. Their outstanding abilities not only enhance how America competes in commerce or contributes to the world in various other ways, it also enhances America's racial image.

Slave descendants who have personal attributes are singled out. They rise in rank and are automatically separated from the average individual slave who cannot add anything to America's advancement. This singling-out is hurtful in many ways, but mostly, it adds to our racial division.

Those descendants of slaves who have the ability to contribute to America could help their people, if they weren't ashamed of who we are. If they were to proudly acknowledge that they are descendants of American Slaves, less fortunate slaves could also take pride in the contributions that *our people* are making to America and to history.

The rest of us are special, too; we just haven't had a fair chance to prove ourselves. Once the white race gets over their shame of slavery and realize that forgiveness can now be achieved, they will be proud of American Slaves, also. How can they not be? They are responsible for us being so special.

Community Pride

Pride and respect go hand in hand. Together, they could clean up our inner cities. For instance: Usually when the police are called to quell a disturbance in our inner cities, as in the case when a descendant of slaves is disturbing the peace, the rowdy individual knows to calm himself or herself, sobered in the knowledge that most police officers in inner cities are licensed to kill. This 'straighten up and fly right' auto-response is due to a fear factor. However, if this same individual were acting up and his minister showed up, he would likewise straighten up. The same response is brought about due to respect, not because of out-and-out fear. Fear and respect can be equally powerful. They can both produce positive results from the same individual for the same offense.

If young inner-city slaves were part of a bona fide, acknowledged people, and if they were acting up and a respected elder of their group showed up, the disorderly slave (or slaves), without a doubt, would straighten up and not a shot would ever be fired. In this hypothetical scenario, he would know that the elder is his senior who does not approve of his actions. Our elders need to get involved again in directing our people, especially our youth. It is because we now fear our young that we aren't letting them know that we disapprove of the pattern of their 'ghetto behavior' in a tone that they will understand and heed.

"Fear and respect can be equally powerful: They can both produce positive results from the same individual for the same offense."

The majority of slaves might have to live in the ghetto, but we must put a stop to the cultivation of ghetto mentalities. I truly believe that if young slaves who misbehave really knew who they were, and could imagine the premeditated hell that our foreparents went through just so we could make it this far, they would change their unacceptable behavior and act decently. I deeply believe if we senior slaves were to solicit our children's help in pulling our nation together, they would be glad to help because it would give purpose to their lives. I understand respect has to be earned, but it also has to be taught, and should be taught — in the home.

The primary reasons our young are following each other is because our Uncle Tom leaders left us behind. We elder slaves stopped leading and started hiding behind closed doors. ❖

CHAPTER 37

America the Beautiful

(But beauty is only skin deep)

Now that I understand America, and the benefits of being an American, I fully understand why members from every nation on earth seek American citizenship. Symbolized by the Statue of Liberty, America opens her "golden door" and says, "Give me your tired, your poor, your huddled masses, yearning to breathe free …"

Yes, America is truly a beautiful land on the outside; however, her inner beauty is tarnished by the ugliness of slavery. The sore of slavery won't stay covered up forever.

Dishonor made honorable

In some cases America is honorable, dignified, and generous, but not necessarily to the descendants of slaves. To show her greatness and prove she truly possesses lofty qualities and is the true champion of freedom, America should *properly* free her only offspring. What better way for America to illustrate to the world she is honorable than to stand dignified as she honors her moral obligation to those who gave so much to her and are willing to give even more. If America were to properly reward those who she owes and has abused, she would have not only shown her generosity, her true integrity would come shining through.

America has turned her back on her only offspring — a people born right here on this land! We are American slave descendants and we love our country, but it is because we are descended from slaves that our country acts as if she doesn't love us. Our ancestors labored many generations without reward. We, the descendants of those slaves, have waited patiently for America to embrace us and be fair toward us, but the past suggests she never will.

The inscription on the Statue of Liberty extends welcome to "the wretched refuse of your teeming shore," but aren't we America's own wretched refuse? If I were to "lift my lamp beside the golden door" and admit openly that I am an American Slave, I fancy it revealing a sign: "Slaves use the colored entrance."

If America doesn't know her obligation to her begotten people, this book is to inform her. If America does know, but doesn't care, this book is to expose her human rights cover-up.

Hopefully, the United States of America is a good mother country; if not, maybe it could become so. Maybe America has been taking care of us in our infancy, by means of welfare, waiting for us to grow up enough to stand on our own. Being an optimist, this is what I prefer to believe.

In any event, we can no longer wait for white folk to think of everything. For American Slaves to evolve properly, our leaders must figure this thing out and start doing their jobs, themselves. Our leaders must form our slave nation into a cohesive body.

The sooner we start, the closer our goal

American Slaves have a natural birth claim to America, but because of our youth we have never had written, racial rules to follow. We have always functioned within the "rules of the land" that were set up to govern free, white people. If for some reason we can't be included in the U.S. Constitution, and if America continues to refuse our slave nation fair and equal treatment, descendants of slaves must

"If I were to 'lift my lamp beside the golden door' and admit openly that I am an American Slave, I fancy it revealing a sign: 'Slaves use the colored entrance.'"

come up with an entirely new set of rules drafted by us, and for us, which will coincide with the rules of the land.

Did you know?

Descendants of American Slaves are the only group in America which doesn't have a Constitution in any shape, form, or fashion. Keep in mind, the American Constitution was initiated by whites, for white Americans only. Other American nationalities have a Constitution in their own country, and this includes true African Americans.

The United States of America boasts being a fair country. Americans give lip service to the concepts of freedom, justice and equality, but America has never been fair to American Slaves. America refuses us freedom, justice, and equality.

When slaves claim merely to be Africans *in any form*, we are allowing America to worm out of her obligation to American Slaves. Denying who we are defeats us. Slaves are what our ancestors were bred to be. Let's face it; that's who they were — we can't change that.

The injustices done to our ethnic community dictate we need, and should be eligible for special care from our government. However, we shouldn't depend solely on that. Our government is controlled by whites, and some in key positions are not sympathetic to the cause of the descendants of American Slaves.

As long as the descendants of American Slaves stay separated we will never advance, which means we will never catch up. Slaves were never taught how to start a continuous communication among ourselves. If someone doesn't realize our condition, our people will always be divided into splinter groups.

Part of any restitution package for slavery should be for America to assist us in coming up with a single institution where the descendants of slaves who need help can receive racial information, direction, or business assistance. This connection point would allow wealthy descendants of slaves to inject money into our racial program, and it would allow wise slaves to instill intelligent input into their own people's mentality. This central control point would be our "giving back" place. It would allow all descendants of slaves to be kept abreast of the state of our culture. If whites were to be instrumental in helping American Slaves organize our group properly and bond to each other securely, this would go a long way in bridging the white/black communication gap.

Time to give back

I have always wanted to give back to my people; however, like other slaves, I didn't understand how to effectively give back to my division of the human race. For years I wasted precious time trying to 'give back' to my people, and it didn't just start when I brought another slave into my manufacturing company and tried to advance him. So, before we put this powerful, often misunderstood and misguided, force into action, let us explore the phrase, "giving back."

"Part of any restitution package for slavery should be for America to assist us in coming up with a single institution where the descendants of slaves who need help can receive racial information, direction or business assistance. This connection point would allow wealthy descendants of slaves to inject money into our racial program, and it would allow wise slaves to instill intelligent input into their own people's mentality."

My giving back started toward the middle of August, 1974. I had been in the grocery business for a while and had just finished building a new food mart. To show my appreciation, I decided to *give back* to my people by throwing a free picnic at Chickasaw Park for the entire West End of Louisville, Ky., which is predominantly black. In ignorance, I spent a bundle of money making sure the music, food, and atmosphere were right. The politicians who attended used the gathering to say all of the right words that would help get them elected or reelected. The people appreciated the picnic, also. That was some time ago.

Since then I have evolved, and now that I look back and visualize who the attendees were and what I was trying to do, which was to 'give back to my people,' I realize that small picnic was just a flash in the pan and of no real significance at all to destitute slave descendants. It didn't even help those Negroes in the neighborhood where my store was located.

After I moved up in status and became a manufacturer, again I wanted to give back to my people. Still in ignorance, I spent a large amount of time, energy, and money trying to help another struggling descendant of slaves develop his tool-and-die business. When we were finished, he could see some daylight, but we had only one small minority business that was *still* struggling. That's when I woke up.

I realized I gave back to an individual, *one person*, which is not the same as helping my people; therefore, I had severely limited my giving. After further scrutiny, I realized, even in this giving back — I could have been giving to the wrong person!

What if this was a selfish person who wouldn't help his people once he escaped poverty? Worse yet, what if his minority business turned out to be a front company? The point is if slaves had a 'giving back place,' we wouldn't be making these harebrained blunders. I wouldn't have wasted good money and precious time accomplishing little. If slaves had a racial nucleus, or a 'hub,' we would have an advancement plan to guide us. There would be people in place to screen out those who would hurt our people and lend a hand to those who would help us. If we had a giving back place, there would be a waiting list of slaves who have good ideas, given talent and individual hopes and dreams that could become solid, viable plans. One of the purposes of such a control point would be to make sure we followed our agreed-upon plan, which would include tying any plans that individual slaves have into our nation's overall, long-term agenda and making sure that slaves get full credit for our peoples' contributions.

Sponsoring a public picnic in a small park did not help our people. Coming back and assisting slaves one at a time, or coming back and helping one business that is owned by a slave, did not work, either. The type of giving back I did is futile. It keeps energetic descendants of slaves spinning their wheels in vain, trying to survive and keep marginal companies alive until help *might* arrive.

I didn't set out just to throw a party in a park, or to help only one person become 'nigger rich.' I really did want to give back to my people. Simply put, I wanted to help my people advance. Without guidance, many descendants of slaves are destined to stumble into the same pitfalls I blindly fell into. I wanted to show my people how to use an escaped slave's stumbling blocks for their stepping stones. I wanted them to understand how to turn my defeats into knowledge that could spell success for them. I felt compelled to take as many of my people as I could by the hand and personally lead them out of the ghetto.

During slavery, there was the 'Underground Railroad.' It was the famous route that slaves took from slavery to freedom. Many descendants of slaves need an 'Aboveground Highway.'

American Slaves are native children of the greatest, commercial country in the world. Therefore, the road we travel has to be above reproach. It must be unrestrained and highly visible. Our immediate goal is to wake up, stand up, and then start growing up with the hope that someday, if we work hard enough and think intelligently, we will be able to assume our rightful, lawful position in America.

Our Aboveground Highway must be very conspicuous and easy to locate. Because it will be the avenue that millions of slaves will take to break away from the poverty that American slavery bred.

I gave at the office

It's true that slaves are an exclusive, easily recognizable group of people, and it's clear to me that we are descendants of slaves. However, because our leaders don't realize this, slaves have to fit in wherever first-class citizens allow us to fit, and then only as imposters.

While coming from a dire background, I have started many businesses and have achieved some modest successes. Because of my experience, I believe I have something to give back to my people but how, and *where can I give back?*

I talked to several wealthy descendants of slaves who could help, and wanted to help, but they said helping one slave advance is high risk, at best. Trying to help every descendant of slaves is impossible and could prove to be dangerous. They made it clear they didn't want to take a chance of upsetting their own lifestyle betting on such unsafe, long shots. One of our high muckety-mucks really got my attention — he said he didn't want to wind up "in a body bag."

The reason these influential slaves have given up trying to help destitute slaves evolve is because the average descendant of slaves doesn't know he needs help, and the rest act like we don't want help — unless it's a handout. I can live with this attitude among the common of our people. They don't know any better. What really bothers me is why haven't our leaders figured out some of these things and started doing something about our racial condition? This should be a leader's mission! All leaders, no matter their ethnicity, have an inherited responsibility to their people first!

If any group of people should be fully included in our country's plan or should want America to be safe and secure, it should be American Slaves. Our retarded state is why America is now quietly, but systematically, almost being taken over by immigrants.

It's a tough job, but ...

I find it difficult to believe that Americans can still be so deliberately callous about something as obligatory as rectifying slavery. America has acquired sophistication, financial strength, knowledge, wealth, world power, and a reputation for getting things done, and slavery was one of the essential building blocks that made these positive features possible.

If the intelligent leaders of both races would come together and communicate properly (which means openly), they could draft a racial, business-related, advancement plan and just "tell it like it is!" Once we think this thing through, we will understand that speaking the truth and then taking our medicine is not so bad; it would heal the wound of slavery. That healing would strengthen our country.

> *"If the intelligent leaders of both races would come together and communicate properly, which means openly, they could draft a racial business-related advancement plan and just "tell it like it is!"*

To speed us on the road to recovery, I recommend a much needed merger between our two peoples. White business-people should welcome this type of merger because they understand the power that merger generates. Because of hardcore ignorance and lack of trust, the average descendant of slaves could balk, and for good reason. Whites have kept slaves, and now their descendants, ignorant with double-talk. Slaves need to understand: What whites regard as legal in the business arena is not necessarily fair in everyday life — but it is "legal." Therefore, what seems wrong to a descendant of slaves can be considered right to whites because, to most of them, *slavery is still just business.* That's the way slave leaders should approach restitution for slavery and also the future of our people because that's what it is, business. ❖

CHAPTER 38

The Birth of a Nation

(Our babies are American bred)

Once the truth surrounding the birth of our slave nation is told openly and without restraint, awareness is going to automatically emerge. When this happens, the inbred ignorance that shrouds America's Slaves will start melting away.

Slaves have known only hypocrisy since their inception; therefore, this particular truth told unflinchingly and without shame, should be similar to the jolt a newborn receives when it is taken from its mother's womb and slapped on its bottom to encourage it to cry the first breath of life. I make this comparison because the American Slaves nation is in the midst of the birthing process.

We're coming out!

If there wasn't permanent mental damage done to our people during our racial incubation, and if our community of people hasn't been in this incubated, ignorant state too long, these written words should cause American Slaves to break free at last. Like a newborn, we will breathe on our own. Our eyes will start opening to the realities of life. This will be the initial awakening of the American Slaves nation.

Now, keep in mind, as the news spreads, there are those who will no doubt try to get our people to focus on the wrong of slavery and the cruelty of whites. This would be an emotional, backward, defeating move. Whites of today didn't have a direct hand in the enslavement of our foreparents; their progenitors did. However, whites of today do have an inherited obligation to eradicate the stain of the sins of their forebears. If today's whites were to help American Slaves be reborn, spiritually and emotionally, and if they were to guide us in our effort to be rejuvenated and developed, this could be the healing balm that would cure the sin of slavery and the many sins committed by the white race during slavery.

Since whites and blacks have no other choice but to live in America together, in harmony, it is up to slave leaders to show whites that 'America' will ultimately be the beneficiary of reparations for slavery. Regardless of our maltreatment, American Slaves are not a vindictive people. My wish is that we stay that way.

First Light

During slavery, slaves were taught to serve the master's needs and were well-trained to run the master's house, his business, his plantation, or whatever. When a thinking leader takes the time to view America, commercially, he will understand right away that this type of dutiful training was a premier education within itself, but we should also understand that those slaves were ignorant. They didn't understand that this was an 'education' nor did they comprehend the importance of this type of learning. When slaves were kicked out of slavery, this 'industrious' education ended, because it was now illegal to work people without pay. Freshly abandoned slaves didn't know the entire slave nation was supposed to build on this 'specialized' education that some of them had received.

The master, being a businessman, kept those slaves who had special skills at his side, because he needed them. Some slaves have always been close to the master, to knowledge and to

American growth. Some of us are still vitally necessary to the stability of the master's house, his business, his 'plantation' — *and our country.*

During slavery, the skill of a few slaves, the ignorance of the majority of slaves, and the callousness of the master, divided slaves into two groups, the field hand and the house nigger. But since then we have evolved into *three* groups. Our foreparents were divided at the initiation of slavery. They were further divided at the ending of slavery: Those slaves the master needed stayed with the master; those slaves the master no longer needed were abandoned.

If today's whites were to help American Slaves be reborn, spiritually and emotionally, and if they were to guide us in our effort to be rejuvenated and developed, this could be the healing balm that would cure the sin of slavery and the many sins committed by the white race during slavery.

Today, there are the 'lesser slaves'; they have no job because they are undertrained, unemployable, and are looked down upon by the next 'higher-class' of slaves who have jobs and are trained. Then, there are the 'upper-class' slaves. They are connected to the system and have what we could call 'good jobs.' They are preachers, politicians, fronts for white organizations, or Uncle Toms in other categories.

Whites are a three-class people, also. The difference is that all classes of whites are free, simply because they are white and whites control America. All classes of slaves are mentally enslaved and always have been. Being divided, we descendants of slaves compete against each other at the lowest level of the American economy and, also, at all levels of the slave nation economy. We hold each other down pulling against each other at all levels.❖

America's Little Black Book

CHAPTER 39

Turning Dream Into Reality

(Learning to crawl)

D r. King informed us that our next battle would be an economic contest. It's only fitting that our business leaders lead us in this fight. It's their job plus they will make a lot of money. For them to be effective, they must have accurate directions, the necessary ammunition, weaponry and intelligence, and a feasible, strong business plan to follow. To construct such a plan, we need our high level leaders to voluntarily come forth and share in a blessed event — the birth of our nation.

"We live in a business environment; therefore, in order for the descendants of slaves to advance, or grow up normally, they must have an advancement avenue, or a growth vehicle to ferry them to their destination, or to maturity."

Slaves should have been recognized and properly formed at the close of the Civil War, but they weren't. This is why we have a very serious task ahead, so we may as well start at the beginning.

Thoughtful deliberation

*T*o help us better understand the overall message, we must now take a comprehensive view of America with the message in mind. We want to visualize how to deliver the Slave nation, secure our future existence in America and, at the same time, ensure a future peaceful coexistence between the white and black cultures.

We live in a business environment; therefore, in order for the descendants of slaves to advance or grow up normally, they must have an advancement avenue or a growth vehicle to ferry them to their destination, or to maturity.

We now understand that America is a business environment; therefore, this mode of conveyance must be a controlled, exclusive business plan. To keep from reinventing the wheel, this plan could be similar, but superior, to America's current Small Business Administration's agenda. This program would become a national control point. Descendants of slaves from across the country could arrange to travel this route to reach the American mainstream.

Those who have ideas that could help smooth the way for American Slaves to enter the American mainstream need to come forth and share. No true American should be excluded from helping us develop. The suggestions I make are business-oriented, and are intended as a business control point as we struggle on the economic battlefield.

It is important that our American Slave program be exclusive, and it calls the descendants of slaves *by name*. Calling the descendants of slaves by name will let us know it is we who are being helped. This will let everyone else know who is being helped, also. Taking this approach, the descendants of slaves, and the world, will know that America has a bona fide program in place to properly compensate the descendants of slaves for the illegal enslavement of their ancestors.

The initiation of a narrowly defined slave program would take the 'reparations heat' off of our government. It would put the burden of reparations for American Slavery squarely on the shoulders of descendants of slaves who are clergy, politicians and business leaders, and rightly so. They are in leadership positions; it's about time they started leading. Once they understand this information, hopefully the rules and regulations of the religious, educational, business, and political environment they function in, and their people live in, will start to become clear. If so, they will learn how the trickle-down theory works in regard to neighborhood economy.

If our political leaders and our clergy will work hand in hand with our business leaders, we can organize ourselves, advance our people, and change the course of our depressing history.

Sounds exciting, and it is. However, in order to turn this exciting dream into the wonderful reality it could and should be and make it beneficial to our people, we must step up voluntarily and start learning how to work together.

Leader, role model, or an Uncle Tom?

It is necessary that those slaves in the public eye realize what is going on around them, comparatively, in order to use their learned experiences effectively. For instance, in the sports arena, there are many black team leaders, black quarterbacks, blacks at every position, and black coaches. Now there are some black sports commentators. The latter sit with the white folks and analyze the game, and they are pretty good, too. They know what is wrong in the game and explain in detail how to fix it. They give particulars of where every player is versus where he should be, what he should be doing, how and why he is doing it. And they all appear to enjoy doing their job. These commentators are descendants of slaves and descendants of slave masters working together.

This can work in other arenas besides merely sports. Why shouldn't whites and blacks work together to help our people? Why aren't those leaders who consider themselves our role models sitting around the conference table analyzing our slave nation in relationship to other American population groups? Why aren't they figuring out workable solutions that will adhere to our special, racial needs?

If African American leaders were to get together, form themselves into a team, and then physically sit at the conference table together after having determined who they *really* are, they should be able to figure out who the rest of us are. The next step would be to figure out what, when, where, how, and who should be involved in our people's advancement.

If we were to take these steps, we could clearly explain our predicament to whites in key positions. Then they would understand which whites should be involved in helping our people. Taking this approach, whites would understand who they are helping and why. I believe they would take pride in helping American Slaves.

My contribution to my people is to write the truth as I receive it. I will then persuade my white associates to help me get the information into print and into the hands of those descendants of slaves who are in leadership and guidance positions. I will tell them that our people need our help — *we must be organized.* Tremendous benefits would become available to our people if we will put our ethnic group in order.

OK, where do we go from here?

Well, because our next battle will be fought on the economic battlefield, we had better plan our strategy. If we were 'at war' in the usual sense we would need a battle plan, but this encounter is not your everyday 'shooting war.' This is an important, sensitive business encounter, sensitive because not too long ago our foreparents were the valuable property that was sold in this arena.

If our plan is sensitive to both cultures and shows why and how it will work to everyone's advantage, I think America will come to our rescue because, to white Americans, it's still just business. And why wouldn't America support our effort to be free once she fully understands who we are? *We're her only begotten* and we've got talent: We just need direction.

Taking our first step

I understand how busy noted descendants of slaves are, but after what our ancestors went through I don't think they would accept "I'm too busy" as a suitable excuse for not helping our people. The birth of a nation of people of common ancestry is a rare occurrence, and it shouldn't be taken lightly.

Summary

*O*nly when descendants of slaves can give directly to our own kind, and this giving helps our entire American Slaves' community, are we effectively giving back to our people. Only when we reach the stage where we have a plan in place that shows us how to help each other and how to rise above the weaker of our people having to wait for white folks' charity, will we have successfully given back.

Realizing the delicacy of the festering slavery situation in America and the violence that followed Dr. King's assassination, it would be foolhardy not to have a legitimate plan in place, and some authentic leaders, in leadership positions, when the masses of slaves start waking up from ignorance and start gaining intelligence. Not only is this the just thing to do, it is the smart thing to do, and should have been done long ago.

Descendants of slaves must understand: Our government is made up largely of decent people who would love to help our segment of the human race. They know American Slaves were abused, and that the descendants of those same slaves are still being discriminated against. However, before our government can help us as a group, our community of people must be identified and then defined.

American Slaves is our proper identity and our true history — *it's our being.* Our name denotes loudly and clearly that we need special help. Will history show that it was the whites of today that truly freed us? It's really their job because they control America, our motherland. White Americans are the true 'parents' of our slave nation.

Whites have a choice: They can do the right thing and help us in our effort to be free and, thereby be recognized as honorable. Their generation then will be recorded in the annals of time as principled citizens who corrected a fault in the fabric of America. History will record that once the defect was recognized and constructive directions were provided, whites took action. If today's whites don't do the right thing, they could be remembered as merely an extension of the cruelty of slavery.

No group of Americans should take this message lightly. American Slaves really do need our nation's help. I understand the "I'd better not get involved because I might offend whites in key positions" attitude; however, this is different in that it involves the future of our people. This might be the only chance our people have at freedom. It is certainly going to be the last chance some of us seniors have to do our part to help save America from continued, covered-up shame and the descendants of slaves from added degradation.

With this knowledge comes an inherited responsibility. It is up to those who have access to TV, radio, and other means of communication, white and black, to spread the word that will alert our masses. Those who possess communication skills must become actively involved.

Now, regarding our senior citizens, white and black, we are those who have been honored with longevity. We might belong to different racial groups, but time has welded us together. We have lived long lives, but separately. Some of us have even flourished. We prospered because we live in America, the country that slaves helped build. We have now reached the 'checkout lane.' We must now ask ourselves: While on earth did we just take up space? Was our longevity just a waste of precious time? Have we truly done our part to make this world a better place? Did we honestly do our best to assist or, in this case, save humanity? Could we have done better?

America keeps watch over the entire world making sure people in other countries are treated fairly and that genocide is not their ultimate fate. If we were to look within our own borders, we would recognize the terrible injustice being dealt out right here at home on the descendants of those who helped build our homeland. I used to wonder why some animals, birds, fish and other wildlife become extinct. I always figured greedy white leaders were the culprit. Now, of course, I realize *they are* because they control the air we breathe and the water we drink. But now, I also realize greedy whites have accomplices — those who lead American Slaves. They are standing by, impassively watching.

When future ecologists and historians tell the American story, what excuse will they use to explain the disappearance of the American Slave? Will they deny that we ever existed, or will they simply shrug and say we are African Americans because we have dark skin?

No matter the color of one's skin, denying facts is a clear sign of ignorance. As Americans, we should be able to rise above. We are Americans, all. Let us not leave this world in a lesser condition than we found it. ❖

INDEX